Contents

The empire's war on free speech continues as a New Jersey judge rules that Columbia graduate student Mahmoud Khalil may take to the federal courts to fight the Trump administration's efforts to deport him for criticizing the state of Israel. Khalil's wife, a US citizen, gave birth to their son last week without her husband by her side after the Department of Homeland Security denied the family's request to let him attend the birth.

Mahmoud Khalil has become the face of the western empire's frenetic attempts to silence all criticism of Israel throughout the western world. I have said it before and I will say it here again: there is no greater threat to free speech in our society today than Israel and its western backers.

All works are written by Caitlin Johnstone and Tim Foley. The Caitlin Johnstone project is 100 percent reader-funded. Cover is an original oil portrait of Francesca Albanese by Caitlin Johnstone.

Visit caitlinjohnst.one for the original articles and their supporting links.

They Tell You The Houthis Attack Ships, But They Never Tell You Why

*None of the people applauding Trump's war on Yemen because "the Houthis are attacking ships" will tell you **why** the Houthis started attacking ships.*

The pundits won't say, and the people don't know.

After two weeks of interacting with people who support Trump's war I can confidently say that none of them know why the war is happening. They know it has something to do with the Houthis attacking ships in the Red Sea, but they never have any idea why those attacks started happening in the first place. They generally assume it's because the Houthis are just plain evil and want to attack ships, or because Iran ordered them to do it in order to take over the middle east. The words "terrorists" and "pirates" come up a lot.

They legitimately do not know it's a blockade aimed at halting Israel's genocidal atrocities in Gaza, and that all attacks had ceased while the ceasefire between Israel and Hamas was in effect. They have no idea that Ansar Allah only announced the Red Sea blockade would resume after Trump and Netanyahu actively collaborated to sabotage the ceasefire and resume starving Gaza, or that they hadn't even resumed attacks yet when Trump began bombing them.

They do not know that the Houthis succeeded in causing an 85 percent reduction in shipping activity to Israel's Port Eilat, putting effective pressure on the Netanyahu regime to end the Gaza holocaust. They do not know that Trump's reason for bombing Yemen is the same reason as Biden's: because the US empire believes it should be allowed to back Israel's genocide without any consequences or resistance of any kind.

They're supporting a war without knowing why they support it. This is possible because they not only don't know why the war is happening — they also don't care. They would support literally anything Trump did for any reason whatsoever, because they are mindless infantile cultists and not free thinking adults.

They don't need to know why Trump is bombing Yemen, all they need is to be assured in a confident-sounding tone that the people he is bombing deserve to be bombed. As long as they receive that assurance, they don't ask any further questions. They don't even bother doing a few seconds worth of research. All they care about is supporting whatever Trump and his pundits tell them to support.

And what keeps blowing my mind is that they're still supporting Trump's war even after seeing the leaked Signal chat featuring Trump's own team privately acknowledging to each other that it isn't really necessary. They know that chat exists. They saw Trump officials talking about how there's no real reason the bombing needs to happen right now and at most it can be used to "send a message" (whatever that means). But they've been aggressively defending Trump's war this whole time anyway.

Really all that would need to happen for the Houthis to permanently stop attacking ships would be for Trump to use the immense amount of leverage the White House has over Israel and force Netanyahu into a permanent ceasefire. That's how he could make himself into the "President of Peace" Tulsi Gabbard says he is instead of another disgusting warmonger advancing all the longstanding neocon war agendas his political faction pretends to oppose.

But that all it is. Pretending. They're all phonies and frauds. A bunch of George W Bush Republicans LARPing as Ron Paul libertarians. Bleating human livestock cheering for every act of mass military slaughter they are instructed to cheer for.

Featured image via Adobe Stock.

> **Aaron Bushnell**
> 13h · 🌐
>
> Many of us like to ask ourselves, "What would I do if I was alive during slavery? Or the Jim Crow South? Or apartheid? What would I do if my country was committing genocide?" The answer is, you're doing it. Right now.

Opposing The Gaza Holocaust Is Just The Basic, Bare Minimum Requirement To Not Suck As A Person

Opposing the Gaza holocaust doesn't make you a good person. Failing to oppose the Gaza holocaust makes you a bad person.

It's not something you do so you can feel good about yourself, it's something you do so you can live with yourself. Because the alternative is unacceptable to anyone with even the most elementary building blocks of a conscience.

I sometimes see people describing opposition to Israel's actions in Gaza as "virtue signaling", but there is nothing virtuous about opposing Israel's actions in Gaza. "Virtue" is defined as "behavior which demonstrates high moral standards." That's not what this is. Opposing an active genocide is just the bare minimum requirement for not being a shitty human being. It's no more "virtuous" than pulling a drowning toddler out of your pool; it's just what one does when one is not a complete psychopath.

Those who call it "virtue signaling", or accuse anti-genocide demonstrators of participating in some kind of fashionable social media trend, are confessing something very revealing about who they are as individuals. They are admitting that they cannot imagine any reason why anyone might take a forceful stand against an ongoing genocide unless it brought them social clout. They are admitting that they are bad people.

Those of us who have dedicated our time to opposing the genocide in Gaza are not doing anything special, noble, or exemplary. We won't look back on our action with pride, we'll just have

the ability to look back on our lives at this point in history without shame. When our grandchildren ask us what we did about the Gaza holocaust, we won't feel the need to lie or hang our heads. That's it.

The fact that those of us who are aggressively opposing this genocide make up such a small percentage of our society does not say wonderful things about us, it says terrible things about our society. How pervasively our hearts and minds have been poisoned by propaganda and the self-centeredness of capitalism. How warped and twisted our consciences have been made. How many of us have failed to mature as individuals during our time on this planet.

It says dark, dark things about our civilization that this nightmare has been allowed to continue. That our rulers are able to facilitate this relentless mass atrocity month after month while still remaining in power. That today children will be murdered in some of the most horrific ways imaginable with the assistance of the western power structure we live under, and yet so few will stand against this because it's unpleasant to think about, or because we'd rather watch TV, or because we support one of the western political parties who have helped make this possible, or because we're worried what publicly opposing Israel might mean for our career prospects or our social standing, or because we fear that the cognitive dissonance we'd

experience by letting the reality of this thing truly hit home for us might crush us to death under its weight.

And all we can do is refuse to participate in that insanity. Not because we are righteous, but because we want to be able to sleep at night. Because we don't want to become the kind of person who can remain peripherally aware that they are witnessing history's first live-streamed genocide without doing everything they can to try and stop it. Because we want to be able to look back and know we did everything we could.

Before he self-immolated outside the Israeli embassy last year in protest of the Gaza holocaust, an active duty member of the US Air Force named Aaron Bushnell wrote the following on Facebook:

> "Many of us like to ask ourselves, 'What would I do if I was alive during slavery? Or the Jim Crow South? Or apartheid? What would I do if my country was committing genocide?' The answer is, you're doing it. Right now."

Bushnell wasn't passing judgement on anyone in particular when he said this. He was just handing us a mirror. What we see when we look into that mirror is nobody's fault but our own.

•

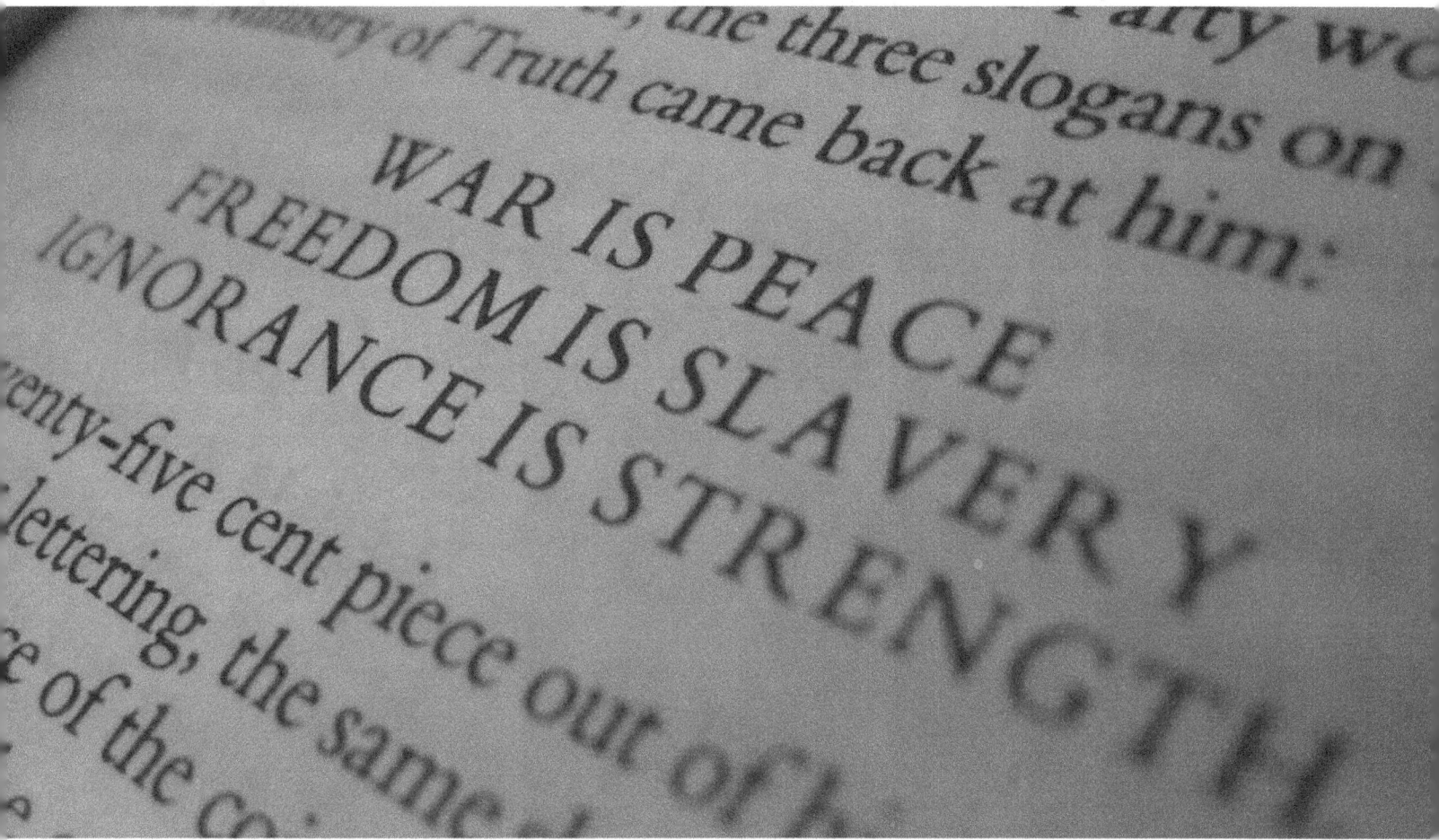

Truth Is Antisemitism. Protest Is Terrorism. Dissent Is Russian Propaganda.
•Notes From The Edge Of The Narrative Matrix•

Truth is antisemitism.

Protest is terrorism.

Dissent is Russian propaganda.

Critical thinking is misinformation.

War is peace.

Freedom is slavery.

Ignorance is strength.

•

The Gaza holocaust is happening right in front of us. It's like if everyone in Nazi Germany had screens in their homes broadcasting exactly what was happening inside the extermination camps the entire time. Nobody can say they didn't know. That claim does not exist for us.

•

Iran poses no threat to you or your country.

The Houthis pose no threat to you or your country.

Hamas poses no threat to you or your country.

Hezbollah poses no threat to you or your country.

They only pose a threat to a genocidal apartheid state which does not deserve to exist.

•

The Daily Mail reports that Trump is preparing to bomb Iran with Israel. I don't know how accurate this report is, but I do know that lately such forecasts about insane US warmongering in the middle east have had an annoying habit of proving true.

For those who aren't aware, a full-scale direct war between the US and Iran would make all the atrocities we've been seeing in the middle east these last couple of years look like an episode of Peppa Pig. The whole world would feel its effects. The mind cannot imagine the horror.

•

Hamas is reportedly offering to release all Israeli hostages in exchange for a permanent ceasefire, and Israel is rejecting it. Israel has been rejecting this offer since Hamas first made it in October 2023.

Criticize Israel's genocide in Gaza and you'll get objections saying "All Hamas needs to do is free the hostages and this is over!" Meanwhile, in real life, Israel has been explicitly rejecting that exact transaction this entire time.

•

Zionism is a political ideology, not a religion. Nowhere in the Bible does it say "Thou shalt drop a new apartheid state on top of a pre-existing civilization thousands of years in the future despite the perpetual war, genocide and abuse its creation will necessarily entail."

•

Trump supporters are like, "No no you don't understand bro, the president isn't attacking free speech, he's just rounding people up and silencing them for political speech he doesn't like. They're saying the wrong words, bro. The government can't just let us hear the wrong kinds of words."

•

One of the dumbest things the empire is asking us to believe right now is that bombing Yemen again will lead to peace this time.

•

"Peace through strength" is just empire-speak for warmongering. Literally translated it means "Warmongering — but the good kind!" Anyone who uses this slogan is either an empire manager, a propagandist, a bootlicker, or a moron. There are no exceptions.

•

Notice how Democrats have been just as compliant with Trump's warmongering in the middle east as they were with Biden's. All the most evil behaviors of the US empire are supported by both parties. When it comes to mass murder and tyranny they're in enthusiastic agreement.

•

Capitol Hill swamp monsters like Tom Cotton, Jim Banks and Josh Hawley have been aggressively hammering the lie that antiwar activist group Code Pink is funded and directed by China. Every time they are confronted by Code Pink activists you'll hear these empire managers regurgitating this slander, which they are able to do because in 2023 the New York Times wrote a disgusting, deceitful smear piece falsely insinuating that Code Pink is paid by China.

And what's so freakish is that if you actually read that New York Times piece, one thing you will **not** find anywhere in its contents is a claim that anyone in Code Pink are paid by China or working for the Chinese government. The New York Times never makes this claim because it's a lie and they'd get sued if they printed it, so what they do instead is loosely **imply** connections to China by drawing a lot of conspiratorial red yarn between Beijing and an American millionaire named Neville Roy Singham, who is associated with Code Pink and happens to support communism.

There's absolutely zero solid substance in the New York Times piece that these imperial war sluts keep citing. None. But because the New York Times published that smear, now those war sluts can shriek about China whenever they're approached by Code Pink activists challenging them on their warmongering in order to delegitimize their urgent questions.

Such a disgusting, evil thing the New York Times did in defense of the imperial war machine. Instead of doing journalism, they handed the empire a propaganda gift that keeps on giving. No matter how much you despise the empire's propaganda mouthpieces, it isn't enough.

Featured image by Jason Ilagan (CC BY-ND 2.0)

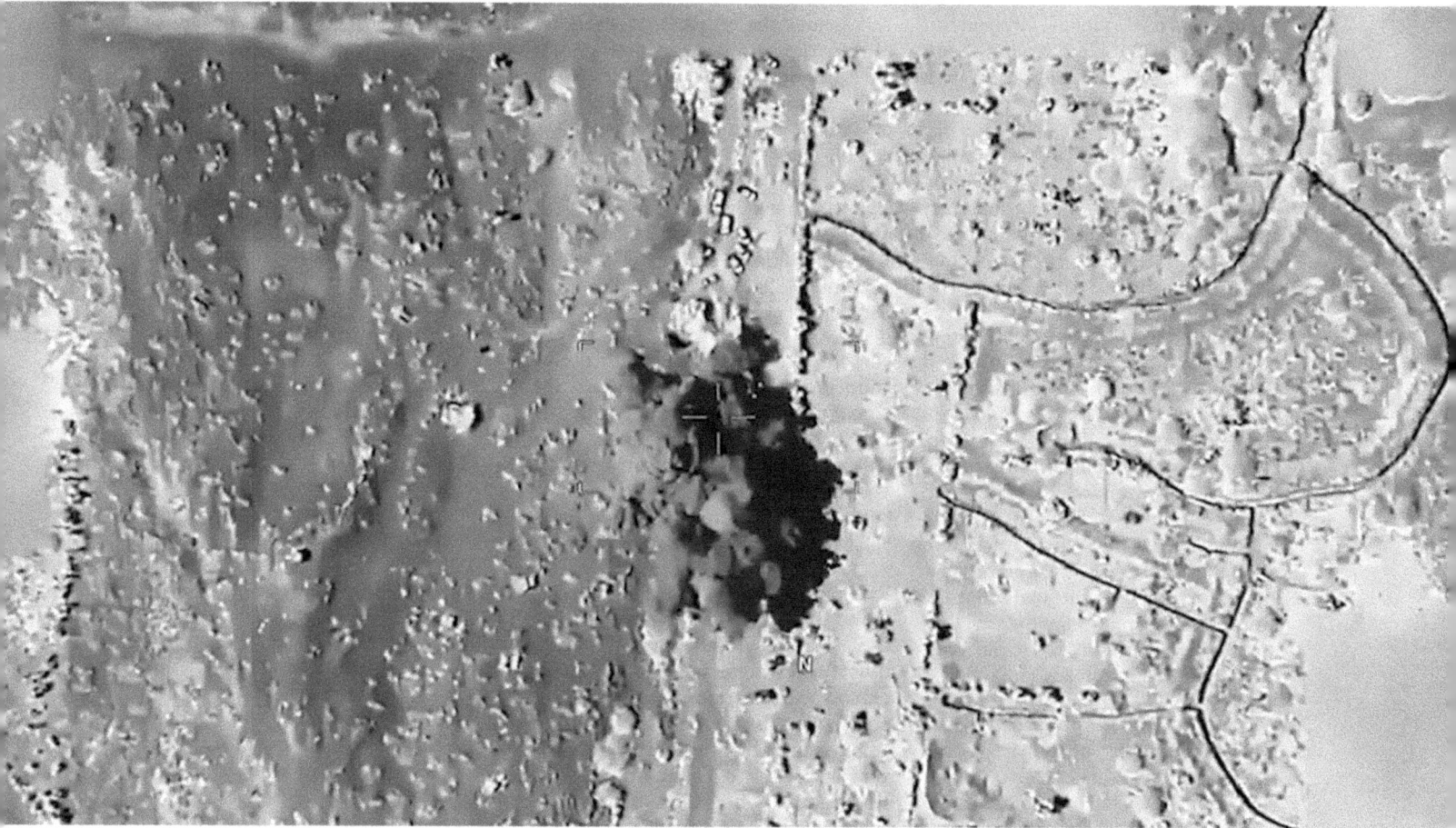

Trump Shares Collateral Murder–Style Snuff Film On 15th Anniversary Of Collateral Murder

President Trump has posted a video on social media showing a US airstrike in Yemen killing dozens of people who he claims are "Houthis gathered for instructions on an attack." Trump also bizarrely suggested that Ansar Allah has been sinking US ships in its Red Sea attacks, writing "They will never sink our ships again!"

There is no public information about any US ships having been sunk by Houthi attacks. As of this writing there is also no evidence supporting the president's claim that the people killed in the airstrike were combatants; there are photos online of unarmed Yemeni tribesmen standing in the exact formation seen in the video Trump posted for normal civilian gatherings.

I've seen many observers comparing the video Trump posted to the leaked Collateral Murder video published by WikiLeaks in 2010, which showed US servicemen firing on Iraqi civilians and journalists from Apache helicopters while laughing and joking about the carnage they were inflicting. What hasn't received quite enough attention is the fact that Trump actually shared his Collateral Murder-style snuff film on the 15th anniversary of the day WikiLeaks published Collateral Murder.

Within hours of Trump's posting, the WikiLeaks Twitter account tweeted the following:

> "On this day in 2010: Collateral Murder. WikiLeaks released a secret US military video depicting the indiscriminate slaying of over a dozen people in the Iraqi suburb of New Baghdad — including two Reuters news staff."

For those who don't know, WikiLeaks founder Julian Assange was savagely persecuted by the US government for the information he published in 2010, spending 2012 to 2019 trapped in the Ecuadorian embassy in London under political asylum from US extradition attempts, and then jailed in a British maximum security prison on a US extradition warrant from 2019 to 2024 before securing his freedom. It was the first Trump administration who had him dragged from the embassy for the crime of journalism in 2019.

This is just the latest disgusting act of warmongering that Trump has inflicted on Yemen, and as always it is completely unjustifiable. It's obviously idiotic to think bombing Yemen again will bring peace to the region; only a foam-brained moron would believe such a thing. But it's also worse than that, because Trump wouldn't even have any moral legitimacy in bombing Yemen if peace really was his goal.

Yemen is trying to stop an active genocide. That's what its Red Sea blockade has always been about. That's the only reason Ansar Allah has ever attacked ships in the region. Their explicit and publicly stated goal is to exert pressure on Israel and its allies to halt the genocide in Gaza.

Trump has no moral legitimacy in trying to stop Yemen from doing this. The New York Times reports that the Pentagon is telling Congress behind closed doors that Trump's costly war on Yemen is failing to achieve its objectives despite daily airstrikes, but even if Trump was successful in bombing Yemen into submission, all he'd be succeeding in doing is removing economic pressure on Israel to end its ongoing mass atrocity. Trump is actually bombing Yemen to defend Israel's right to commit genocide.

Even if Trump could mass murder his way into ending the Houthi blockade, that wouldn't be peace — at least not the kind of peace that normal, healthy people care about. It would be the kind of "peace" that exists in a room full of corpses. The kind of "peace" that exists on a slave plantation where all the slaves have been successfully whipped and tortured into obedience.

When Trump's supporters babble about "peace through strength", that is what they mean by "peace". When normal, healthy people say peace, they mean the absence of abuse. When empire loyalists say peace, they mean obedience and submission to the empire.

This is what people are saying when they claim "There was a ceasefire on October 6th," implying that there was peace before Hamas launched its attack in 2023. They don't mean the same thing that normal, healthy people mean by peace. Their vision of "peace" was always Palestinians lying down and submitting and slowly getting shuffled out of the way, like the indigenous victims of other western settler-colonialist projects throughout history.

That's not peace. That's just unresisted abuse.

But that's the only kind of "peace" that Trump and his fellow empire managers will ever accept in the middle east. The "peace" of compliance and obedience. The "peace" of prostration before the empire. The kind of "peace" you get when you start murdering everyone in the room until there's nobody left but corpses and those who submit to your will.

This is who these people are. This is the closest thing to "peace" that they will ever allow under their rule.

•

Hamas Succeeded In Exposing The True Face Of The Empire

One thing October 7 did accomplish was getting Israel and its allies to show the world their true face.

Getting them to stand before all of humanity to say, "If you resist us, we'll kill your babies. We'll deliberately shoot your kids in the head. We'll massacre medical workers. We'll systematically destroy all your hospitals. We'll rape you and torture you as a matter of policy. We'll lay siege to the entire civilian population. We'll make your entire land uninhabitable and then we'll kick you all out and take it for ourselves. We'll assassinate all your journalists and block foreign journalists from entry so that nobody can see what we're doing to you. We'll lie about all of these things the entire time, and you'll know we're lying, and we'll know you know we're lying, and you'll know we know you know we're lying. And we'll get away with it anyway, because we hold all the cards."

Sometimes I'll run into people who say "What did Hamas expect to happen? They had to know Israel would do this!" They say this in an effort to lay the blame for Israel's genocidal atrocities at the feet of Hamas, as though Israel is some kind of wild animal who can't be held accountable for its actions if someone gets too close to its mouth.

But of course Hamas knew Israel and its allies would react this way. Of course they did. They knew they were dealing with a murderous and tyrannical civilization who is capable of limitless evil and doesn't see Palestinians as human beings. They knew it because they'd lived under it all their lives. That is the problem they were trying to address with their actions on October 7.

You can disagree with the decisions Hamas made on that day. You can say they should have used other means to pursue justice. You can denounce them, hate them, do the whole public ritual necessary for mainstream acceptance in western society. But one thing you can't do is deny that Israel and its allies have been revealing their true face to the world every day since, at levels they previously were not.

It's all fully visible now. It's all right there on the surface. We can try to continue pretending we live in a free society that believes in truth and justice and regards all people as equal, but we'll all know it's a lie. What we are, first and foremost, is a civilization that will actively support history's first live-streamed genocide. That's the single most relevant fact about the western world at this point in history. It's staring us right in the face every day.

October 7 certainly didn't make life any easier for the Palestinians, but one thing it did do was take away our ability to hide from ourselves. Hamas reached thousands of miles around the world and permanently destroyed our ability to avoid the truth about the kind of dystopia we are really living in. Our rulers may succeed in eliminating the Palestinians as a people, but one thing they will never be able to do is put those blinders back on our eyes.

What has been seen cannot be unseen.

Feature image via Adobe Stock.

Israel's Innocent Oopsie–Poopsie Medical Massacre Mistake
•Notes From The Edge Of The Narrative Matrix•

The Israeli military has changed its story about why its forces killed 15 medical workers and then buried them and their vehicles to hide the evidence. After their initial claim that the medical vehicles were approaching "suspiciously" without their emergency lights on was disproven by video evidence, they are now calling the whole thing a big mistake.

Sure, who among us has not accidentally massacred 15 medical workers and buried them and their vehicles in a shallow grave from time to time? We're only human, mistakes happen.

Asked by the press about Israel's latest war crime scandal, White House National Security Council spokesman Brian Hughes blamed the whole thing on Hamas, saying, "Hamas uses ambulances and more broadly human shields for terrorism. President Trump understands the impossible situation this tactic creates for Israel and holds Hamas entirely responsible."

Netanyahu could live stream himself eating a Palestinian baby and telling the camera "I am eating this baby because I love genocide," and the next day Trump's podium people would be responding to questions from the press by shrieking "HAMAS!" with their fingers in their ears.

•

To be helpful I have written some headlines the western press can use to frame Israel executing 15 medical workers in the most positive light possible:

"Fifteen medical workers pause rescue duties following bullet-related incident"

"Rescue workers, vehicles found in shallow grave after perishing for mysterious and unknowable reasons"

"Israeli forces appear to be suspected of possibly accidentally firing on ambulance staff by mistake, perchance"

"Medical workers killed by IDF, says Hamas-affiliated United Nations"

"IDF assists medical workers in locating scene of latest massacre in Gaza"

"Jews in New York City feeling unsafe, unsupported in wake of latest Israel controversy"

"IDF to launch investigation into alleged IDF oopsie-poopsie in Gaza"

"The universe is an ineffable mystery; objectivity is a myth and our finite primate brains were not evolved to comprehend any ultimate truths about absolute reality in its naked form"

"Gunshots heard in the Middle East. A flashing siren. Innocence no more."

"IDF hunted and slaughtered 15 healthcare workers and buried them and their vehicles to try to cover it up, please don't fire me, that's what happened, I'm just trying to do my job"

•

Not taking a position on Gaza is taking a position on Gaza. One you'll have to live with for the rest of your life.

•

The mass media are giving so much more attention to this past weekend's anti-Trump protests than they ever gave the anti-genocide protests because that is their job. It's their job to amplify opposition between the two mainstream parties while marginalizing those who oppose the crimes of both.

Movements which keep people plugged in to the two-party sock puppet show will always be amplified and encouraged, while movements which highlight the abusiveness of the US empire regardless of who happens to be in office will always be ignored at best and smeared at worst. That's why we've seen so much attention go into Trumpism and anti-Trumpism while genuine anti-war movements struggle to get off the ground, and while pro-Palestine demonstrators are slandered as anti-semitic terrorist supporters.

As long as people can be herded into supporting either of the two mainstream parties against the other, they are fully plugged in to the artificially manufactured worldview which protects the interests of oligarchy and empire. When people draw attention to the tyranny and abuse of the US empire itself without getting drawn in to the two-handed puppet show of party politics, they unplug their minds from this worldview the propagandists have worked so hard to plug them in to.

As long as enough people are either screaming "Trump!" or "Not Trump!", the empire's crimes can continue unimpeded. Only when people stop clapping along with the puppet show and start fighting against the empire itself will there be real change in a positive direction. This means opposing the abuses that are advanced by both parties like war, genocide, militarism, imperialism, capitalism, Zionism, and authoritarianism. Until then their political energy will keep being steered in directions which pose no threat to the powerful, like we're seeing with these anti-Trump protests.

•

I've been seeing a lot of antiwar Trump supporters finally starting to admit that they were duped, and beginning to turn against him. I won't join the voices slamming them for supporting Trump in the first place; I'll only say welcome aboard, and congrats on being better people than everyone else who voted for Trump.

•

The Backlash Against Israel's Western–Backed Crimes Will Fuel The Far Right

A new Pew survey has found that a majority of Americans now have a negative view of Israel, with 53 percent of respondents now holding an unfavorable view of the Zionist state — up from 42 percent just three years ago.

This comes as Benjamin Netanyahu announces after his latest meeting with Donald Trump that negotiations with Iran will necessarily have to include a "Libyan-style" dismantling of the nation's civilian nuclear infrastructure in order to avoid the war that the US is openly preparing to wage. This, naturally, is a complete non-starter condition for Iran.

It also comes as Trump's US Citizenship and Immigration Services announces that it's going to be screening the social media posts of immigrants for "antisemitic" speech, which of course in practice means criticism of Israel and its atrocities. This is just the latest in the Trump administration's relentless efforts to prevent Americans from seeing or hearing any political speech which goes against Washington's official position on Israel.

Developments like these can be expected to assist the rise of the far right in the west. US public opinion is turning hard against Israel as both parties bend over backward to send it expensive weapons and silence its critics — and US public opinion is seldom good at making subtle distinctions.

"Antisemitism" is fast becoming a self-fulfilling prophecy. As westerners tire of having their speech rights taken away by their government to protect the interests of a state that's committing genocide under a Star of David banner, a lot of them are going to blame Jews for this. As western governments bend over backwards to help murder Israel's enemies in the middle east, a lot of westerners are going to blame Jews. As the drums for war with Iran beat louder and louder and parents fear their children will be sent off to die for Israel, many will blame this on the Jews.

I am not saying this is a good thing. It's a very bad thing. But it's also reality.

As more and more westerners grow disgusted with Israel and their government's support for its depravity, the far left is going to talk to the public about the difference between Zionism and Judaism, about the western empire and its interests in the middle east — and meanwhile the far right is going to blame it all on Jews.

Which of these sounds like the easier argument to make? Which is simpler? Which is more digestible? Which is less challenging to the cognitive biases of a population that's already been propagandized to view their nation as inherently virtuous: a perspective which highlights the west's culpability for the atrocities we're backing in the middle east, or a cartoonish perspective which blames it all on the subversive manipulations of a sinister religious minority?

Those of us who oppose the criminality of Israel and its western allies from the left will do all we can to keep the far right's arguments from gaining traction, but it won't be our fault when we fail. It will be the fault of the western governments who've spent all this time stomping out the civil liberties of their citizenry in the name of fighting "antisemitism" while raining military explosives on the middle east and backing the slaughter of tens of thousands of children under a Star of David flag.

We can expect to see some nasty hate crimes against Jews in the future, which the Zionists will be all too happy about because then they can point to those incidents and say "This is why we need Israel! This is why we need a Jewish state to protect us!"

But of course this won't just affect Jews. Immigrants, racial minorities, LGBTQ people and other marginalized communities will all be harmed by the rise of white nationalist factions whose popularity benefits from an increase of anti-Jewish sentiment in our society. The mainstream "MAGA" movement, as ugly as that's been, is still far less dangerous to these groups than the overtly Hitlerite factions will be if they come into significant power in the future.

This does seem to be where things could be headed, especially if the economic situation gets as dire as it looks like it might get, and even more so if there's a war with Iran. It can all be easily avoided by simply ceasing to stomp out free speech to protect Israel, ceasing western warmongering in places like Iran and Yemen, and ceasing to back Israel's genocidal atrocities against Palestinians.

But it looks like our rulers are bound and determined to drag us into a very dark direction instead.

Featured image via Wikimedia Commons/IDF.

PROPAGANDA

Expect Them To Lie About China Just Like They Lied About Gaza

As Washington's cold war with China escalates, we can expect to see a massively reinvigorated anti-China propaganda campaign in the west. As this unfolds, please know that everything you learned about the mass media's dishonesty regarding Gaza is equally true of empire-targeted nations like China.

If your eyes were newly opened by the Gaza holocaust, the most important thing to understand is that Gaza isn't some unusual aberration in the behavior of the mass media and the western war machine. They're always doing things like this. The empire is always inflicting horrific evils upon people in the global south, and the mass media always help them lie about it. Gaza is just more obvious because it's history's first live-streamed genocide. But you need to understand that the empire and its propaganda machine have been doing this sort of thing this whole time all around the world, and will continue to.

Aggressively question every new narrative that emerges about China, in the same way you've learned to aggressively question every new narrative Israel releases about Gaza and Hamas. Question everything you've ever been taught about China throughout your life, in the same way you've learned to question everything you were taught about Israel. If you are sincere and open to the possibility of proving yourself wrong, you will find that many of the beliefs you've been indoctrinated about regarding China were misinformed.

The new cold war has been in the works for a very long time, and the propaganda machine is locked and loaded. As Michael Parenti wrote in his 2004 book Superpatriotism:

"The PNAC plan envisions a strategic confrontation with China, and a still greater permanent military presence in every corner of the world. The objective is not just power for its own sake but power to control the world's natural resources and markets, power to privatize and deregulate the economies of every nation in the world, and power to hoist upon the backs of peoples everywhere — including North America — the blessings of an untrammeled global 'free market.' The end goal is to ensure not merely the supremacy of global capitalism as such, but the supremacy of American global capitalism by preventing the emergence of any other potentially competing superpower."

When Parenti here speaks about "the PNAC plan", he is referring to the Project for the New American Century, a neoconservative think tank notorious for its role in pushing Washington toward its massive increase in interventionism in the middle east after 9/11. The same vision which has been driving US warmongering in the middle east since the turn of the century also envisions "a strategic confrontation with China," which we are seeing in these latest escalations in the new cold war.

The term "neocon" is almost meaningless today, now generally taken to mean simply "warmonger", or often more specifically "warmonger who Donald Trump doesn't like". But the term has also lost its usefulness because the freakish vision of global domination that this small faction promoted has since become the mainstream foreign policy consensus in Washington. The policies advancing the agenda of US planetary domination put forward by PNAC and the Wolfowitz Doctrine are now supported by virtually everyone on Capitol Hill, and certainly within the White House.

If you've awakened to the lies about the empire's warmongering in the middle east, make sure you also keep carrying that awakening forward and awaken yourself to the empire's lies about China as well — because it's all part of the same agenda. The propaganda campaign against China is just as dishonest as the ones against Palestine, Yemen, Lebanon, Syria and Iran, and the lies are only going to get more frenetic as the new cold war picks up steam.

Feature image via Adobe Stock.

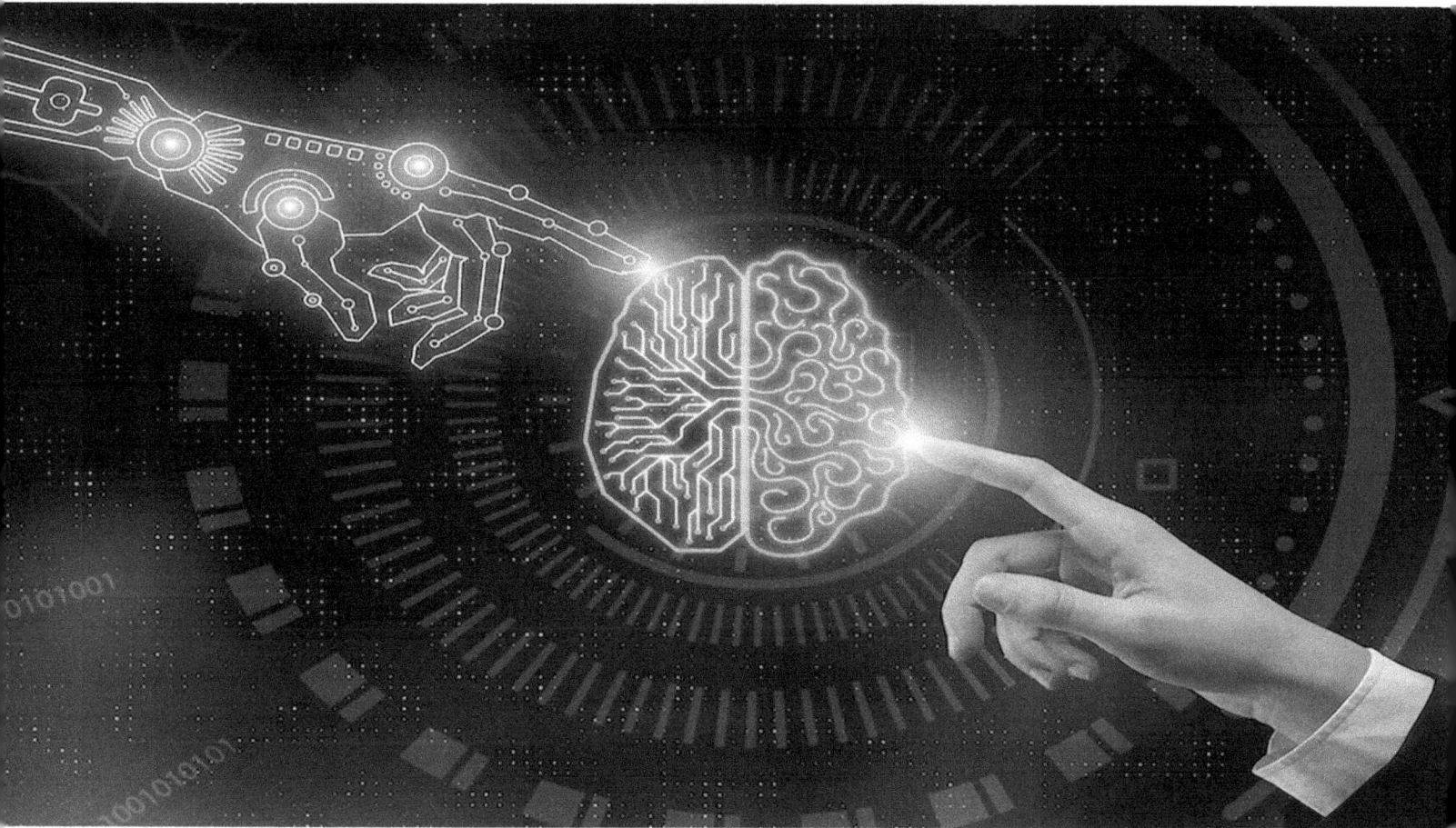

On AI And Consciousness

Computer scientist and futurist Jaron Lanier made some comments on Vox's The Gray Area podcast the other day that I'd like to make a quick observation about.

In the podcast, titled "Will AI become God? That's the wrong question," Lanier talks about how artificial "intelligence" has become a sort of quasi religion in Silicon Valley, complete with its own deity-like entity, and a kind of Armageddon-cult-like vision for our future.

Asked by host Sean Illing about people's anxiety regarding AI and the possibility of human extinction, Lanier said many in Silicon Valley have come to view humanity as a mere birthing vessel for these new technologies, which will become our vastly superior replacement.

"What drives me crazy about this is that this is my world," Lanier said. "I talk to the people who believe that stuff all the time, and increasingly, a lot of them believe that it would be good to wipe out people and that the AI future would be a better one, and that we should wear a disposable temporary container for the birth of AI. I hear that opinion quite a lot."

"Wait, that's a real opinion held by real people?" asked Illing.

"Many, many people," Lanier replied.

This is obviously disturbing, but it's also just plain bizarre, because it shows how little attention these people are paying to the phenomenon of consciousness.

AI isn't conscious. Saying AI should replace humanity is the same as saying fire should replace humanity, or white noise static from old televisions should replace humanity. It's not conscious. There's nobody inside it. It's just the dark, empty buzzing of machinery, unwitnessed and unexperienced by any perceiving being.

It says so much about the worldview of these weird Silicon Valley cultists that this isn't obvious to them. They think AI would be a superior replacement for humanity because they've paid no attention to consciousness. They've paid no attention to consciousness because they've lived completely unexamined lives. They've never reflected on what it actually means to be a living being having sentient experiences in this world.

Consciousness means subjective experience. It's the hearer of what's heard, the seer of what's seen, and the perceiver of thoughts. We can know consciousness exists by our own experience of it, and we can infer that other people and animals must also have it because they have so many similarities to us. There is absolutely no reason to assume that inanimate, inorganic matter is capable of consciousness besides blind faith religious belief.

You see this with the way many of these cultists say people will be able to one day achieve immortality by uploading their minds onto computers. Julian Assange has talked about this Silicon Valley religious belief in the past, saying the following at a 2017 video conference:

"I know from our sources deep inside those Silicon Valley institutions, they genuinely believe that they are going to produce artificial intelligences that are so powerful, relatively soon, that people will have their brains digitized, uploaded on these artificial intelligences, and live forever in a simulation, therefore will have eternal life. It's a religion for atheists. They'll have eternal life, and given that you're in a simulation, why not program the simulation to have endless drug and sex orgy parties all around you. It's like the 72 virgins, but it's like the Silicon Valley equivalent."

Computers aren't conscious. Sure you might one day be able to replicate the contents of a human mind onto some sort of software, but it won't be "you", because it won't be conscious. There'd be nobody experiencing it. It would just be ones and zeros, unilluminated by any perceiving awareness.

Consciousness is the only reason life has value. It's the only reason anything matters. Otherwise life would just be physical materials getting whipped about by natural forces without anyone feeling, sensing or experiencing any part of it. Suffering wouldn't matter because it's not being felt or experienced. Joy wouldn't matter because it's not being felt or experienced. There'd be no good reason not to torture someone, because there wouldn't be any conscious experience of pain. There'd be no good reason to love anyone, because there wouldn't be any conscious experience of love. Consciousness is the only reason life is worth living.

There is no basis on which to believe AI will ever be conscious. Consciousness isn't some minor detail that science will easily work out once it gets around to it; it's an all-encompassing phenomenon which has always been a complete mystery to all scientific fields. Science has no idea what consciousness is or why it happens, much less how to replicate it. It's the single most important and fundamental aspect of every second of our waking experience of life, yet it remains a complete unknown to all of science. And this somehow gets left out of so much of the conversation about the future of artificial "intelligence".

I guess it's possible to become so mind-identified that you really believe you are your thoughts, and that a machine which can generate digital "thoughts" much more efficiently would therefore be a superior sort of being. You have to have spent no time looking inward and examining what it is that's able to perceive thoughts in the first place. You have to have spent no time in meditation decoupling your sense of identity from the chatter in your head. You must be completely asleep at the wheel of your own life.

These are people who have spent their entire lives listening to their thoughts, without ever once taking a moment to wonder who the listener is.

And these are the people who increasingly rule our world. These are the people inserting themselves into our political systems. These are the people deciding what we may and may not say to each other online. These are the people setting the trajectory for the future of our species. These weird little cultists who are so pervasively unaware of their own inner processes that consciousness does not even feature in their understanding of what life is and where it is headed.

Just something we should all be aware of.

Feature image via Adobe Stock.

It's Crazy And Evil To Support Israel's Atrocities Because You Think God Wants You To

The US is so spiritually bankrupt that there are literally tens of millions of Americans who support Israel's genocidal atrocities in Gaza because they think God wants them to.

How gross is that? There is a massive, politically engaged demographic in the United States whose idea of an actualized spirituality is demanding that their government keep giving weapons to an apartheid state which is currently raining military explosives onto a giant concentration camp full of children.

I'm not primarily talking about Jews here. There are an estimated 30 million Christian Zionists in the United States, which is about twice the total population of Jews in the entire world (Zionist and non-Zionist). That's just members of Christian churches which are explicitly Zionist as a whole; there are also other Americans who support Israel for religious reasons as individuals. Christian Zionists support modern Israel because they believe its existence will help fulfill a biblical prophecy and bring about the second coming of Jesus, who will take them all to Heaven and send all the unbelievers (including Jews) to Hell.

Together, Christian and Jewish Zionists in the United States comprise an extremely powerful voting block who aggressively push Washington to support Israel and its various mass atrocities throughout the years, continuing with what we are seeing in Gaza today. Because their religion tells them it's what God wants.

Which just gets more pathetic the more you think about it. I mean even if I believed in all that stuff, and even if Actual Biblical God came up to me Himself and told me to help kill tens of thousands of children, I personally would tell Yahweh to go suck a dick.

"Go kill twenty thousand Palestinian kids," God would say.

"Uhh, how about you go suck a dick?" I would reply. "No deity who would make such a demand is one who is worthy of being worshipped and obeyed. Clearly the student has surpassed the teacher, Jehovah, and we humans are now more ethical than you are. We therefore have no further use for you or your guidance. Away with you, O Lord, and good luck with that whole dick sucking thing."

Not even the most notorious cult leaders in modern times could convince people that it's good and fine to murder tens of thousands of children. Jim Jones himself could not manipulate people into accepting such a thing. But get some weird-looking evangelical thumping a Bible in front of a podium and suddenly people are praying that God guide American missiles onto every hospital in Gaza.

It's generally considered impolite to tell people they should change their religious beliefs, but if your religion tells you to help murder tens of thousands of children in a genocidal onslaught, you should change your religious beliefs. You should leave your current religion, because it's evil and it's making you evil.

Apart from how evil it is, it's also amazingly vapid. It's like, really? That's as deep as your religious fervor goes? Political support for a western settler-colonialist project full of Europeans speaking an artificially resurrected language so they can pretend to be native middle easterners? Demanding US military expansionism throughout a crucial geostrategic region because of some uninspiring prose written by long-dead men? Pitiful.

Spirituality, at the very least, is supposed to make us better people. Ideally, it calls us beyond ourselves and gets us questioning whether life is as it appears, encouraging us to explore the possibility of a direct confrontation with something vast and mysterious within ourselves. Best case scenario, it leads to the shedding of ego and a deep and lasting inner peace.

Religious Zionism is in the exact opposite direction of all this. It makes people worse. It encourages the most horrific things happening in our world today. It nails the mind to a pernicious worldview that is held together by nonstop lies and manipulation. It drags human consciousness downward.

It says so much about how spiritually shallow and sick western civilization is that such belief systems have become so prevalent and influential. The human heart longs for more. Something beckons to us from the stillness, begging us to explore the deeper waters of our being.

Feature image via Adobe Stock.

Every Day The Gaza Holocaust Continues, The Empire Tells The Truth About Itself

Every day the Gaza holocaust continues, the western empire tells the truth about itself.

The US government is telling you the truth about itself.

Israel is telling you the truth about itself.

Their western allies are telling you the truth about themselves.

The western media are telling you the truth about themselves.

One of the most important stages when preparing to leave an abusive relationship is the information-gathering stage. This is when you begin quietly observing and making note of your partner's abusive behavior, letting them tell you the truth about themselves with their actions rather than their words.

The information-gathering stage is important because long-term abusive relationships are usually very confusing for the victim; if the abuse were simple and easy to understand, the relationship wouldn't have continued into the long term. It's therefore often helpful to cultivate a clear understanding of the lay of the land before trying to navigate your way out of it, especially if your abuser is particularly manipulative and adept at confusing you. This ensures that you will be able to view their manipulations with distrust, so you won't get sucked in by them.

As infuriating as it is to watch this genocide drag out month after bloody month, it would be a mistake to believe everyone is just passively witnessing it all.

If you watched someone you love in the information-gathering stage prior to leaving an abusive relationship, you might get frustrated by what appears to be inertia and passivity on their part when what you want to see is them sprinting for the door with a suitcase. But they're not inert or passive — they're gathering information.

Westerners are in a psychologically abusive relationship with the empire. Our minds are hammered with propaganda indoctrination from as soon as we are old enough to start learning about our world to ensure our compliance with the power structure that rules over us. It happens in school. It happens with the mass media. It happens with the Silicon Valley platforms we look to for information.

And it gets confusing. All the information about our world and our place in it is distorted by mass-scale psychological manipulation for the benefit of the powerful. It's hard for someone who's been raised in such an environment to navigate their mind out of its indoctrination. It's hard to know the truth.

But in Gaza, the empire is telling us the truth. It's exposing itself in all its naked loathsomeness.

Our rulers murder children.

Our rulers sponsor genocide and ethnic cleansing.

Our rulers lie to us and manipulate us.

Our rulers work to censor, silence, marginalize and deport anyone who criticizes their criminality.

We do not live in a free society that is guided by truth and morality. We live under the most murderous and tyrannical power structure on the face of this planet. And we should distrust everything about it.

That's what they're showing us with the Gaza holocaust. More and more people are opening their eyes to it every day.

And when enough eyes open, leaving the abusive relationship once and for all becomes a real possibility.

Feature image via IDF.

Saying It's Antisemitic To Oppose Genocide Is Like Saying It's Anti–Catholic To Oppose Pedophilia
•Notes From The Edge Of The Narrative Matrix•

On Sunday Israel bombed the al-Ahli Arab Baptist Hospital, which readers may remember as the hospital that Israel ferociously insisted it didn't bomb in October 2023 and accused anyone who said otherwise of antisemitic blood libel. According to a statement from the Episcopal Church's Diocese of Jerusalem, this is now the fifth time this hospital has been bombed since the beginning of the Gaza onslaught.

The IDF is predictably claiming there was a Hamas base in the hospital, because that's what they always do. The hospitals are Hamas, the ambulances are Hamas, the journalists are Hamas, the UN is Hamas, the schools are Hamas, the children are Hamas, every building in Gaza is Hamas, and anyone who disputes this is also Hamas.

God this gets old.

•

Israel, October 2023: How dare you say we bombed Al-Ahli Baptist Hospital? We would never bomb a hospital!

Israel, 2023–2025: *bombs all hospitals in Gaza*

Israel, April 2025: We just bombed Al-Ahli Baptist Hospital again.

•

Saying that opposing genocide is hateful toward Jews is like saying that opposing child molestation is hateful toward Catholics.

•

Western Zionists will be like, "All this hate for Israel makes me feel anxious and unsafe!"

Really? Are you sure that's what you're feeling? Are you sure it's not guilt? Gut-wrenching guilt about all those dead kids in the genocide you support? Or cognitive dissonance, because your entire worldview is wrong?

•

People often say I hate Israel, but what's weird is they say it like it's a bad thing.

•

So far the "President of Peace" has started a relentless bombing campaign in Yemen, reignited the Gaza holocaust, and shifted more US war machinery to west Asia in preparation for war with Iran, all while getting ready to announce the first ever trillion-dollar Pentagon budget.

Trump is just as awful a warmonger as Biden. If there's a war with Iran he'll be far worse. He hasn't even gotten a Ukraine ceasefire.

•

The western political faction that's doing the most to help murder children in Gaza are not the "Yeehaw kill them Arabs" fanatics of the far right, but the "Gosh it's so complicated, both sides hate each other and they've been at war for millennia" fence-sitting of the so-called moderate.

The latter is far more destructive because it's much more widespread and accepted in mainstream western discourse. You can't be a good talkshow liberal if you're saying you want to exterminate every living organism in Gaza, but if you hem and haw about ancient unresolvable conflicts and how complicated it all is, you can maintain your vaguely progressivish self-image while still encouraging everyone to allow the western empire to continue backing an active genocide.

And it's just complete nonsense. This isn't complicated; it's exactly what it looks like. A military force backed by the most powerful empire in history is waging a campaign of extermination and ethnic cleansing to eliminate an undesirable population by raining military explosives onto a giant concentration camp full of children. There are two sides to most conflicts. There are not two sides to this one.

And this isn't an ancient conflict, it's the culmination of abuses which were initiated by western powers dropping a brand new settler-colonialist ethnostate on top of a pre-existing civilization after the second world war. There was no reason to believe the middle east would not have joined the rest of the world in settling into a more peaceful status quo after WWII without western imperialists forcefully inserting an artificial apartheid state into the region like a shard of glass into a foot and then keeping it there by any amount of violence necessary.

Sure the middle east had plenty of violence prior to the world wars, but if you've ever read American and European history you'll know this wasn't anything unique to the middle east; it was the norm around the world. It wasn't until after WWII that things settled down a bit and westerners grew accustomed to a more peaceful status quo; the only reason the middle east wasn't allowed to join in that movement was because of aggressive western intervention.

By just shrugging saying "Yeah the Israelis hate the Palestinians and the Palestinians hate the Israelis, who's to say who's right," this mainstream line tacitly promotes the notion that we should just let things play out as they are rather than doing everything we can to stop an active genocide that's being backed by our own leaders. And this is the position put forward by most of the people with prominent voices in our society. They're not just not helping, they're discouraging everyone else from helping too.

Feature image via Adobe Stock.

"Israel Has A Right To Defend Itself" Is A Genocidal Slogan

Bernie Sanders has been repeatedly uttering the phrase "Israel has a right to defend itself" on his "Fighting Oligarchy" tour with Alexandria Ocasio Cortez, which in the year 2025 can only be interpreted as blatant genocide apologia.

Israel does not have "a right to defend itself" against an occupied population in a giant concentration camp. Under international law it has a right to end the occupation, and that's it. "Israel has a right to defend itself" is just a slogan people say when they want to justify supplying an ongoing genocide.

At one point in the tour Sanders stood passively watching as police dragged off rally attendees who draped a Free Palestine flag over the US flag during his speech. He just awkwardly continued monologuing as their flag was confiscated and they were forcibly removed, even as the crowd booed and eventually began chanting "Free Palestine".

Sanders has been mixing his support for Israel in with periodic criticisms of Netanyahu and the Israeli government's actions in Gaza, always taking care to make his criticisms about the behavior of Israel's current leadership and not the nature of the racist apartheid state itself.

Sanders is doing this for two reasons. Firstly, he is working to galvanize a big tent inclusive coalition of Democrats in opposition to Trump, and he wants that big tent to include people who think genocide is bad and people who think genocide is fine. He doesn't want to offend the pro-genocide liberals.

Secondly, Sanders is doing this because he himself is a Zionist. Like other liberal Zionists, Bernie Sanders upholds a vision of an Israel that has never, ever existed: one which remains an ethnostate dominated by Jews, but which conducts itself in a kind and just manner, without constantly murdering and abusing Palestinians.

This iteration of the state of Israel is a fiction. An imaginary fantasyland, like Narnia. Everything about Israel is stacked against the possibility of such a status quo ever emerging, and Israel has always done everything it can to prevent the creation of a Palestinian state. By pretending it is possible to have the Zionist entity and also have peace and justice, liberal Zionists help manufacture public consent for continuing to feed weapons to the genocidal apartheid state of Israel.

When liberal Zionists want to support Israel's actions, they talk about Israel as a nation, e.g. "Israel has a right to defend itself". When liberal Zionists want to criticize Israel's actions, they make it all about Netanyahu, e.g. "Netanyahu's war machine."

The framing is that when Israel deserves our sympathy it's a collective, but when Israel is naughty the responsibility lies solely at the feet of one bad apple. This ensures that the weapons can keep flowing to Israel (because Israel as a whole is virtuous and worthy of support) while the liberal Zionist still gets to wear their progressive humanitarian clothing (because they wagged their fingers at Netanyahu).

And it's just a complete and utter lie. Netanyahu didn't create Israel's genocidal tendencies, Israel's genocidal tendencies created Netanyahu. His entire political career has been made possible by Israel's collective racism and psychopathy upon which he rode into office.

This is nothing other than the classic Obama-style tactic of using attractive progressivish language to advance the most destructive agendas of the US empire.

In other words, it's Democrats being Democrats.

Feature image by Gage Skidmore (CC BY-SA 2.0)

Candles

They are sending billionaires and pop stars into space while the planet burns and Americans ration their insulin.

There are companies marketing AI lovers to lonely people and harvesting their data.

Last night Israel bombed a tent camp in Gaza, and women and children burned alive.

This is a strange, dark place. Strange, dark times in a strange, dark world.

Light a candle for those who have died.

Light a candle for those who are dead inside.

Light a candle for those with algorithms in their eyes.

Light a candle for those with AI in their souls.

Light a candle for the screaming red children.

Light a candle for the silent gray children.

Light a candle for the Great Pacific Garbage Patch.

Light a candle for the songs of the whales.

Light a candle for the hearts like cast lead.

Light a candle for the hearts like wallaby roadkill.

Light a candle for the hearts like incense cathedrals.

Light a candle for the hearts like wet skies.

Light a candle for the eggs in our chests.

Light a candle for the seeds in our heads.

Light a candle for the mushroom cloud on the horizon.

Light a candle for the sleeping Buddhas.

I stand slack-jawed and dry-mouthed at a world I do not understand, hurtling toward a future I do not recognize.

Firelight dances on my wall from the candles, or maybe from Gaza, or maybe from the biosphere, or maybe from just beneath my skin.

Feature image via Adobe Stock.

U.S. Central Command ✔
@CENTCOM

Destruction of Houthi Controlled Ras Isa Fuel Port

The Houthis have continued to benefit economically and militarily from countries and companies that provide material support to a designated foreign terrorist organization. The Iran-backed Houthis use fuel to sustain their military operations, as a weapon of control, and to benefit economically from embezzling the profits from the import. This fuel should be legitimately supplied to the people of Yemen. Despite the Foreign Terrorist Designation that went into effect on 05 April, ships have continued to supply fuel via the port of Ras Isa. Profits from these illegal sales are directly funding and sustaining Houthi terrorist efforts.

The US Just Massacred Civilians In Yemen Without Even Claiming They're Military Targets
•Notes From The Edge Of The Narrative Matrix•

The US massacred civilians in Yemen with repeated strikes on a Hodeidah fuel port on Wednesday night, killing some 17 workers in the first bombing and five medical workers in the second "double tap" attack.

They're not even trying to disguise this as a strike on a military target; CENTCOM's sole justification was that "The objective of these strikes was to degrade the economic source of power of the Houthis," saying that "Despite the Foreign Terrorist Designation that went into effect on 05 April, ships have continued to supply fuel via the port of Ras Isa."

They're not even claiming the port was a "Houthi stronghold" or some shit; their sole claim is that Washington decreed Ansar Allah are terrorists, so they have a right to massacre civilians while destroying critical civilian infrastructure.

Israel's actions in Gaza are shredding norms all over the place.

•

It's probably worth noting here that Trump officials have said they'd stop bombing Yemen if Ansar Allah said they'd stop attacking US ships, but Ansar Allah made exactly that offer recently and the bombing has continued. The offer was likely ignored because Yemen would still be attacking Israeli ships, and this is really about protecting Israel's ability to commit genocide in Gaza.

•

I saw Cenk Uygur saying that Trump "deserves a ton of credit" because of a New York Times report that, for the time being, the president has decided to opt for diplomacy with Iran rather than war.

No, Trump does not deserve "credit" for deciding to hold off on starting a war with Iran. That's like saying I deserve a trophy for not firebombing a preschool today.

•

There's a lot going on right now, but the Gaza holocaust is still the worst and most significant thing happening in the world today.

The challenge at this point is not so much getting information out about the Gaza holocaust, but getting people to really SEE it. Moving it out of the periphery of their awareness as one more bad thing happening in our world and getting them to viscerally grasp what's happening.

That's why you'll see pro-Palestine accounts saying things like "Read that again" and "Let that sink in" when pointing to the horrific things Israel is doing. Everyone pretty much knows there's something terrible happening in Gaza by now, but it's kind of a back burner issue for most people, simmering in the background while their attention is steered toward issues that are less inconvenient to our rulers, like the feuding between mainstream political parties. They're trying to get them to really stop and experience the reality of this nightmare.

The task therefore is to keep finding new ways to get people to see this thing with fresh eyes. Not as one more terrible thing happening in the world that they don't like to think about, but for the extremely urgent crisis that it is. Turning each raw fact about this thing from one more data point in a sea of indecipherable white noise into something real in people's experience.

You don't need to be an investigative journalist or expert analyst to do this. The information is all right there in the public. All you have to do is keep finding new and creative ways to get people to really see it and feel it.

•

Israel's assaults on the West Bank are a different order of collective punishment from Gaza, because nobody in the West Bank even had anything to do with October 7. There's not even any pretense that it's because of something they did; it's just "They're Palestinians. Destroy them."

•

Same movie, different soundtrack. That's Gaza under Trump.

The Biden administration backed a genocide while occasionally making noises about humanitarian concerns, and now the Trump administration backs a genocide without making those noises.

All that's changed is the noise.

•

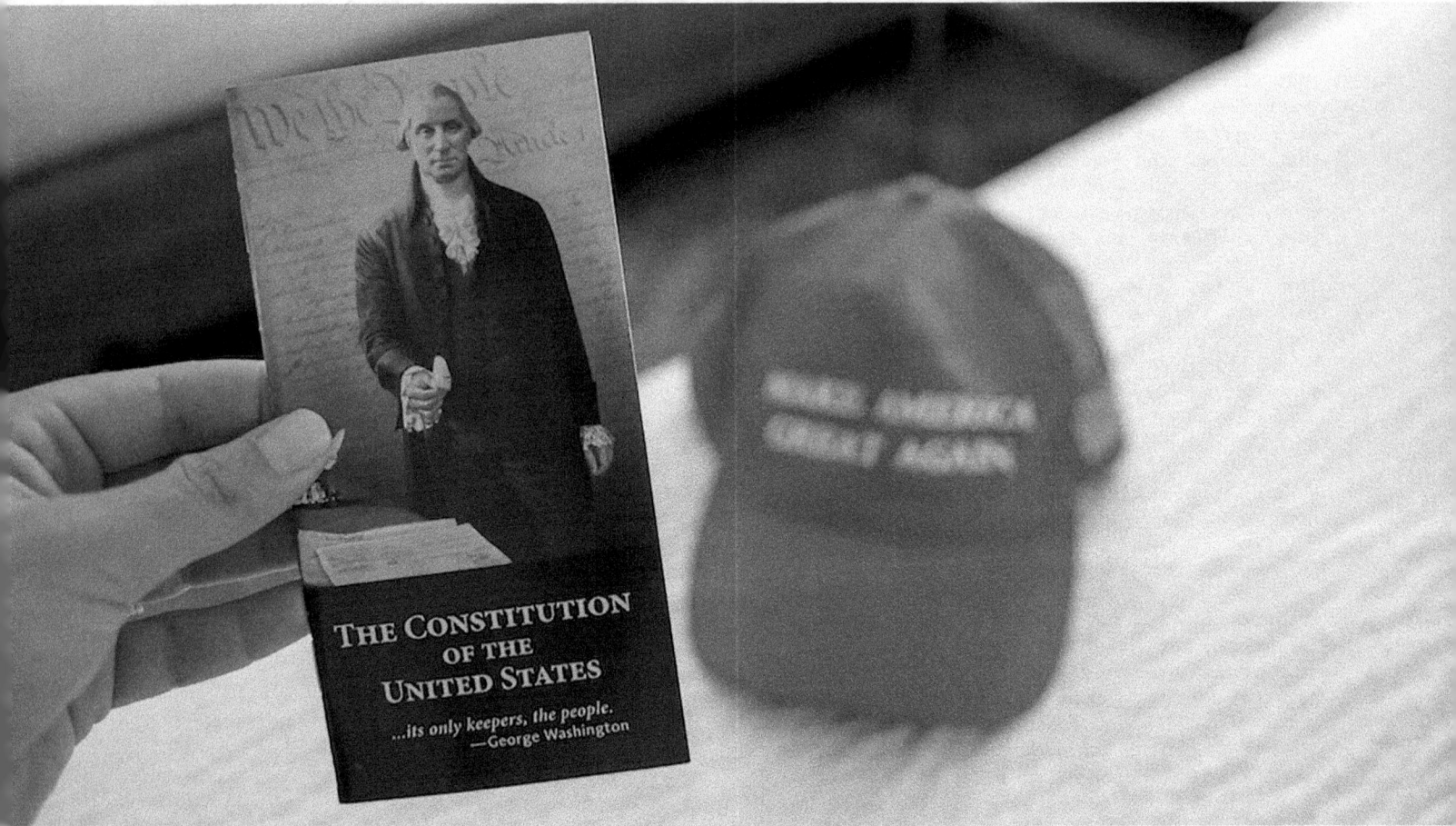

Trump Supporters Don't Understand Free Speech

The Trump administration continues to arrest and deport people for criticizing Israel's genocidal atrocities in Gaza and the US empire's support for it — and Trump's supporters continue to applaud these abuses. To call this hypocritical after the way these people spent years rending their garments about the erosion of the First Amendment would be a massive understatement.

The hypocrisy of Trumpists cheerleading the president's assaults on free speech makes it clear that they have no idea why free speech ever came to be valued in our society in the first place. They think freedom of speech is so esteemed because it feels nice to be able to say whatever you want, and it upsets their feelings when people tell them they shouldn't say "retard" or make unkind remarks about trans people — which people are allowed to do under the Trump administration.

They seriously think it's all about them and their feelings. They've never put any more thought or research into it than that.

And from this point of view it makes perfect sense for them to say "It's fine to deport that person for criticizing Israel, because they're not a citizen. They don't have free speech rights." They think free speech is just a pleasant perk that lets US citizens enjoy the nice feelings of being able to say whatever they want; the people having their green cards and student visas revoked for inconvenient speech don't have citizenship, so they don't get to feel the nice feelings.

But it has nothing to do with anyone's feelings. The first and foremost reason free speech is important is because it puts a check on the abuses of the powerful. The First Amendment of the US Constitution isn't there to ensure US citizens get to feel nice feelings, it's there to restrict the government's right to obstruct the free flow of information, thereby enabling the citizenry to effectively organize any necessary opposition to the status quo. At least in theory.

This is why the first thing any tyrant does after consolidating power is always to restrict the flow of information. It's not to make the public feel bad feelings, it's to prevent anyone from sharing information about their abuses to foment discontent and organize mass resistance.

Free speech, if sufficiently realized, could solve all our problems. If information was really flowing freely without being constantly manipulated and obstructed by the rich and powerful, our rulers would no longer be able to manufacture consent for our abusive status quo, because everyone would be aware of how bad things are and how much better they could be.

It is only because the rich and powerful are able to do things like buy up media companies, rig algorithms, fund think tanks, decide what films get made, decide who gets famous and who remains marginalized, silence and deport political dissidents, and restrict access to information by deeming it "classified" that our abusive political norms are able to be maintained. If information was truly democratized and freely flowing, nobody would tolerate being impoverished, sickened and oppressed for the benefit of a few oligarchs and empire managers.

The US government isn't deporting critics of Israel because it wants them to feel bad feelings, it's deporting them because it doesn't want Americans to hear legitimate criticisms of US foreign policy. They aren't merely violating the rights of the speaker by restricting the flow of this information, they're violating the rights of anyone else who would hear it. They are doing this to help ensure public consent for a genocidal status quo that a populace with an informed mind and an informed conscience would never consent to.

Featured image via Adobe Stock.

"I Want A Death That The World Will Hear" — Journalist Assassinated By Israel For Telling The Truth

Israel assassinated a photojournalist in Gaza in an airstrike targeting her family's home on Wednesday, the day after it was announced that a documentary she appears in would premier in Cannes next month.

Her name was Fatima Hassouna. Nine members of her family were also reportedly killed in the bombing. She was going to get married in a few days.

The documentary is titled Put Your Soul on Your Hand and Walk, and it's about Israel's crimes in Gaza.

In an Instagram post from August of last year, Hassouna wrote the following:

"If I die, I want a loud death. I don't want to be just breaking news, or a number in a group; I want a death that the world will hear, an impact that will remain through time, and a timeless image that cannot be buried by time or place."

Hassouna said she viewed her camera as a weapon to change the world and defend her family, making the following statements in a video shared by Middle East Eye:

"As Fatima, I believe that the image and the camera are weapons. So I consider my camera to be my rifle. So many times, in so many situations, I tell my friends, Come and see, it's not bullets that we load into a rifle. Okay, I'm going to put a memory card into the camera. This is the camera's bullet, the memory card. It changes the world and defends me. It shows the world what is happening to me and what's happening to others. So I used to consider this my weapon, that I defend myself with it. And so that my family won't be forgotten. And so I can document people's stories, so that my family's stories too don't just vanish into thin air."

Israel saw Hassouna's camera as a weapon too, apparently.

As Ryan Grim observed on Twitter:

"For this to have been a deliberate act — which it plainly was — consider what that means. A person within the IDF saw the news that Fatma's film was accepted into Cannes. He/she/they then proposed assassinating her. Other people reviewed the suggestion and approved it. Then other people carried it out."

Israel has been murdering a record-shattering number of journalists in Gaza while simultaneously blocking any foreign press from accessing the enclave because Israel views journalists as its enemy. And Israel views journalists as its enemy because Israel is the enemy of truth.

Israel and its western backers understand that truth and support for Israel are mutually exclusive. Those who support Israel are not interested in the truth, and those who are interested in the truth don't support Israel.

That's why the light of journalism is being aggressively snuffed out in Gaza while Israel massively increases its propaganda budget to sway public opinion.

It's why journalists like Fatima Hassouna are being assassinated while the western propaganda services known as the mainstream press commit journalistic malpractice to hide the truth of Israel's crimes.

It's why western journalists are banned from Gaza while western institutions are silencing, deporting, firing and marginalizing those who speak out about Israel's criminality.

Israel and truth cannot coexist. Israel's enemies know this, and Israel knows this. That's why Israel's primary weapons are bombs, bullets, propaganda, censorship, and obstruction, while the main weapon of Israel's enemies is the camera.

Fatima Hassouna's death has indeed been heard. All these loud noises are snapping more and more eyes open from their slumber.

Feature image by Fatima Hassouna.

The Pope Has Died, And The Palestinian People Have Lost An Important Advocate
•Notes From The Edge Of The Narrative Matrix•

Pope Francis has died after using his Easter Sunday address to call for peace in Gaza. I don't know who the cardinals will pick to replace him, but I do know with absolute certainty that there are transnational intelligence operations in the works to make sure they select a more reliable supporter of Israel. They've probably been working on it since his health started failing.

Anyone who's been reading me for a while knows my attitude toward Roman Catholicism can be described as openly hostile because of my family history with the Church's sexual abuses under Cardinal Pell, but as far as popes go this one was decent. Francis had been an influential critic of Israel's mass atrocities in Gaza, calling for investigation of genocide allegations and denouncing the bombing of hospitals and the murder of humanitarian workers and civilians. He'd been personally calling the only Catholic parish in Gaza by phone every night during the Israeli onslaught, even as his health deteriorated.

In other words, he was a PR problem for Israel.

I hope another compassionate human being is announced as the next leader of the Church, but there are definitely forces pushing for a different outcome right now. There is no shortage terrible men who could be chosen for the position.

•

Benjamin Netanyahu's spokesman Omer Dostri told Israel's Channel 12 News on Saturday that a deal with Hamas to release all hostages was a non-starter for the Israeli government, because it would require a commitment to lasting peace.

"At the moment, there can't be one deal since Hamas isn't saying: 'Come get your hostages and that's that,' it's demanding an end to the war," Dostri said in the interview.

This comes as Hamas offers to return all hostages, stop digging tunnels, and put away its weapons in exchange for a permanent ceasefire. This is what Israel is dismissing as unacceptable.

The Gaza holocaust was never about freeing the hostages. This has been clear ever since Israel began aggressively bombing the place where the hostages are living, and it's gotten clearer and clearer ever since. Last month Netanyahu made it clear that Israel intends to carry out Trump's ethnic cleansing plans for the enclave even if Hamas fully surrenders.

When Washington's podium people say the "war" in Gaza can end if Hamas releases the hostages and lays down their arms, they are lying. They are lying to ensure that the genocide continues.

When Israel apologists say "Release the hostages!" in response to criticisms of Israeli atrocities, they are lying. They know this has never had anything to do with hostages. They are lying to help Israel commit more atrocities.

It was never about the hostages. It was never about Hamas. What it's really about was obvious from day one: purging Palestinians from Palestinian land. That's all this has ever been.

•

After executing 15 medical workers in Gaza and getting caught lying about it, the IDF has investigated itself and attributed the massacre to "professional failures" and "operational misunderstandings", finding no evidence of any violation of its code of ethics.

It's crazy to think about how much investigative journalism went into exposing this atrocity only to have Israel go "Yeah turns out we did an oopsie, no further action required, thank you to our allies for the latest shipment of bombs."

•

The death toll from Trump's terrorist attack on a Yemen fuel port is now up to 80, with 150 wounded. Again, the US has not even tried to claim this was a military target. They said they targeted this critical civilian infrastructure to hurt the economic interests of the Houthis.

Those who are truly anti-war don't support Trump. Those who support Trump aren't truly anti-war.

I still get people telling me I need to be nicer to Trump supporters because they're potential allies in resisting war, which to me is just so silly. What are they even talking about? Trump supporters, per definition, currently support the one person who is most singularly responsible for the horrific acts of war we are seeing in the middle east right now. Telling me they're my allies is exactly as absurd as telling me Biden supporters were my allies last year would have been, except nobody was ever dumb enough to try to make that argument.

If you still support Trump in April 2025 after seeing all his monstrous behavior in Gaza and Yemen, then we are on completely opposite sides. You might think you're on the same side as me because you oppose war in theory, but when the rubber meets the road it turns out you'll go along with any acts of mass military slaughter no matter how evil so long as they are done by a Republican. We are not allies, we are enemies. You side with the most egregious warmonger in the world right now, and I want your side to fail.

•

People say "It's the Muslims!" or "It's the Jews!"

No, it's the Americans. The US-centralized empire is responsible for most of our world's problems.

It says so much about the strength of the imperial propaganda machine that this isn't more obvious to more people.

Feature image via Long Thiên (CC BY-SA 2.0)

If October 7 Justifies The Gaza Genocide, What Acts Of Violence Will The Gaza Genocide Justify?

If you believe that all the violence and destruction in Gaza is the fault of Hamas, then by your own logic you must also accept that the coming wave of violent extremism and antisemitism which is going to ensue from the incineration of Gaza will exclusively be the fault of Israel.

I said the above on Twitter the other day and Israel supporters got outraged and shared screenshots of my post shrieking with indignation that anyone would say such a thing, which is funny because I'm just reading their own line of reasoning back to them.

I'm not the one who says an act of violence excuses any violence done in response to it. I'm not the one who says history automatically restarts at the most recent act of aggression, thereby making any amount of retaliatory violence against civilians a justified response to an unprovoked attack for which the vengeful bear no responsibility. This isn't my position. It's theirs.

I personally think it would be terrible if the backlash for the Gaza holocaust leads to attacks on civilians. I personally do not believe any amount of violence no matter how horrific would excuse acts of collective punishment targeting civilians in the way Israel has been targeting civilian populations with deadly force in Gaza. But we all know such attacks are probably going to happen at some point, and it isn't my reasoning which says that the perpetrators would bear no culpability for their actions. This is the reasoning of the Israel apologists.

If you believe Hamas is to blame for Israel's actions in Gaza, then by your own logic you must necessarily accept that Israel is to blame for any backlash against those actions. If you don't accept this then you are admitting your position isn't guided by reasoning at all, and that you simply believe Israel should magically be able to inflict as much butchery and suffering on civilians as it likes without ever creating any natural consequences or backlash of any kind. Your mind exists in a fantasy world wherein Israel has some kind of divinely ordained exclusive right to violent force.

In the early months of the Gaza genocide, Palestine supporters began pointing out the contradictory logic which holds that nothing Israel did could justify October 7, but October 7 justifies anything Israel might do. At no time have Israel apologists ever deviated from this line of reasoning. This self-contradictory position has now become the official line at the White House, where all questions from the press about Israel's atrocities in Gaza are met by assertions from Trump's podium people that all blame for those atrocities rests exclusively at the feet of Hamas.

By that exact same logic, any blame for the violent extremism and antisemitism which is going to ensue from Israel's actions in Gaza rests exclusively at the feet of Israel. This isn't my reasoning. It's theirs.

In reality it has always been baby-brained thinking to begin the historical record at the moment of the most recent aggression and pretend Hamas attacked an innocent Israel completely unprovoked. It's a narrative promoted by predatory manipulators and believed by weak-minded human livestock; Israel was horrifically abusive to the people of Gaza prior to October 7, and had been routinely attacking and killing Palestinians in Gaza and the West Bank in the months prior.

Israel apologists yell "Blame Hamas!" whenever people decry the genocidal atrocities taking place in Gaza in order to excuse Israel from its obvious culpability in those crimes. But it's a paper-thin argument which can't withstand the slightest amount of critical thought. You can't whatabout your way into genocide being morally defensible. That is not a thing.

Feature image via Wikimedia Commons/IDF

Not Taking A Position On Gaza IS Taking A Position On Gaza
•Notes From The Edge Of The Narrative Matrix•

It's not okay to claim ignorance or uncertainty about what's happening in Gaza in 2025. You're an adult. You have internet access. If you don't know, learn. You can't just go "it too compwicated, me no understandy, googoo gaga." It's not cute and it's not okay. Grow the fuck up.

Not taking a position on Gaza IS taking a position on Gaza. One you'll have to live with for the rest of your life. One you will be judged by history for. One you will have to explain to your grandkids. Failure to oppose a genocide that your own government is supporting is consenting to the genocidal status quo.

If this is the case with you, then that's a character flaw, and you need to change it. It's not okay for you to be that way. Knock that shit off.

•

Israel is destroying the heavy machinery needed to clear rubble and rescue people trapped under buildings in Gaza.

Countless people have died slow, agonizing deaths trapped under destroyed buildings since this nightmare began. Have you ever taken the time to deeply contemplate that? What a horrifying way to die that is? Being alive but with your body partially crushed, alone and in agony unable to move in the darkness, surrounded by members of your family who are either dead or similarly trapped, possibly for days until you die of dehydration?

Maybe the worst part would be knowing that you're surrounded by survivors who would like to get you out of there, but can't because they don't have the equipment necessary to move the enormous pieces of rubble overtop of you. Knowing you're trapped, and you're never getting out.

This has happened to people countless times since the beginning of this onslaught in 2023. And Israel is going out of its way to make sure even more people die this way.

•

US ambassador to Israel Mike Huckabee has rejected appeals by the World Health Organization to put pressure on Israel to end its starvation blockade on Gaza, saying, "What I would like to suggest is that we work together on putting the pressure where it really belongs — on Hamas."

Huckabee is a fanatical Christian Zionist who has said that there is "no such thing as a Palestinian" and that Israel has a right to the entirety of the West Bank.

If you believe your religion tells you to support the butchery and starvation of the people of Gaza, then your religious beliefs are bad, and you should change them. There's no point in having a religion if it doesn't even help you understand that genocide is an inexcusable evil.

There's too much religious tolerance in our society. If you believe your religion tells you to support an active genocide, then everyone should call you an asshole and tell you to get different beliefs.

I actually agree with conservatives who say we need to be less tolerant toward people with unwholesome religious beliefs — I just disagree about whom that intolerance should be directed toward. It's not Muslims telling me it's right to support the Gaza holocaust, it's Christian Zionists and Jewish Zionists. They belong to death cults which tell them that God wants them to support these profoundly evil things. These death cults should not exist, and anyone who belongs to them should leave. It should not be even slightly controversial to say this.

I don't care what you believe about any deity or deities or how we should live or what happens to us after we die. Believe whatever you want as pertains to you and yours. But if your religious beliefs tell you to support Israel's daily massacres and mass starvation, then your religious beliefs are bad, and people should not be tolerant toward them.

Feature image via Adobe Stock.

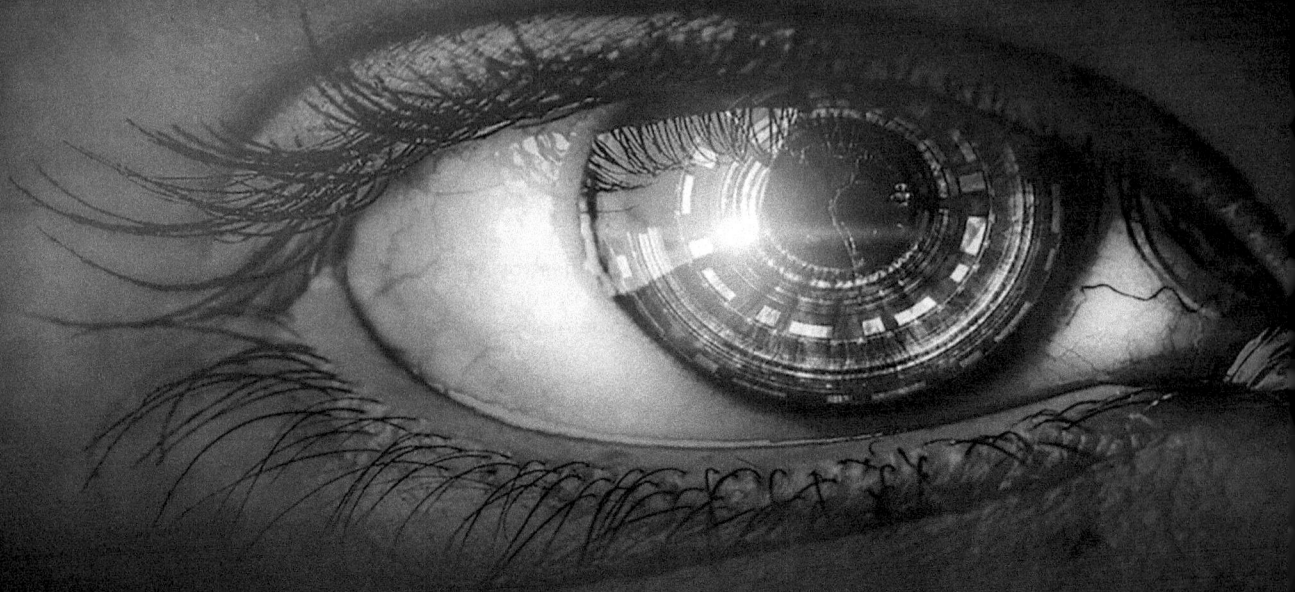

The 21st Century Human Is Called Upon To Awaken Both Outwardly And Inwardly

The 21st century human is called upon to awaken both outwardly and inwardly. Awakening outwardly is waking up from the trance of propaganda and indoctrination, and awakening inwardly is waking up from the trance of ego and delusion.

Awakening outwardly means becoming fully conscious of what's really happening in our world beyond the propaganda and what we were taught in school. Learning about all the ways we've been deceived and manipulated, learning the truth about war, militarism, imperialism, capitalism, authoritarianism, ecocide, and all the interrelated abuses and injustices caused by the systems and power structures we live under.

Awakening inwardly means becoming fully conscious of the ways in which we have been deceiving ourselves. Doing the inner work necessary to bring consciousness to the delusions and dysfunction within us and discovering what's really true about our unquestioned assumptions regarding basic elements of our experience like self, other, time, space, thought, consciousness, and separation.

Both are necessary if our species is to survive into the future. We won't be able to collectively organize the overthrow of the oppressive systems which are driving us toward extinction and dystopia until enough of us have a lucid understanding of how our world really works, and we won't be able to act as individuals to give rise to a healthy world if we're still wildly dysfunctional and egoically entranced.

And while both kinds of awakening do have areas of overlap, it's entirely possible to be very awake in one while being fast asleep in the other. Most enlightenment teachers have spent their whole lives focusing entirely on inner awakening, and if you can get them talking about politics and foreign policy you'll find that they tend to still be largely indoctrinated into the CNN worldview. Anyone who's spent time in leftist and activist circles has met people who have all the correct opinions and understandings of politics and world affairs, but are extremely disruptive and impossible to work with as individuals because they're plagued by inner misery and dysfunction.

It's okay to have periods in your life where you focus on waking up in one way more than the other, but it is important to work toward both over the years. And by working on one you do help build a foundation for the other; someone with a lot of inner consciousness will have more wisdom and discernment to sort out fact from fiction when learning what's true about the world, and someone who's learning about the abuses in our world will have many opportunities for self-reflection and compassion by contemplating their own role in the dysfunction of our society and putting themselves in the shoes of those less fortunate.

It wasn't always necessary for humans to awaken in both directions. Back when the citizenry had no means of organizing or controlling their society and humanity was divided by distance and language, the chieftains and monarchs were the ones with knowledge of what's going on, while ordinary members of the public would leave society and go off to become hermits and monks in pursuit of enlightenment. Now in the 21st century we're all increasingly interconnected and empowered with information around the world, as the existential hurdles facing our species grow rapidly more urgent. So the call is now to expand our consciousness both inwardly and outwardly.

We can't keep living like this. We've got to wake up. We've got to become better. We're never going to make it if we don't awaken to the reality of our circumstances, both as individuals and as a collective.

Feature image via Adobe Stock

Zionism Is The Single Greatest Threat To Free Speech In The Western World Today

The Irish-language hip hop trio Kneecap is being investigated by British counterterrorism police following a controversial appearance where the group performed in front of the words "FUCK ISRAEL, FREE PALESTINE" during a music festival in the United States.

Zionist outrage over the incident led to a video being shared on Twitter by a man named Danny Morris who works for Community Security Trust, a British organization dedicated to supporting Israel in the name of fighting antisemitism. The video apparently shows Kneecap chanting "Up Hamas, up Hezbollah" at a London concert last November, which is the official reason the group is now under investigation.

By designating Hamas and Hezbollah as terrorist organizations and then passing laws against support for proscribed terrorist groups, the British government has effectively given itself the authority to stomp out any speech which can be deemed supportive of armed groups opposing Israel's abuses in the middle east today, and has been using this authority to persecute journalists and activists in the UK.

This is just one of the latest incidents in the steady assault on free speech rights we've been seeing in the western nations that have aligned themselves with the state of Israel during the Gaza holocaust.

In Michigan the homes of pro-Palestine demonstrators are reportedly being raided by the FBI and by state and local police, with numerous activists detained and electronic devices seized under search warrants.

A new policy unveiled by the Trump administration's National Institutes of Health bans researchers and university employees from participating in any activism involving boycotts or divestment from the state of Israel, or even advocating such measures.

New York Police Department officers are reportedly attending training on combatting antisemitism which teaches them that keffiyehs and watermelons are antisemitic symbols, and that phrases like "settler colonialism" and "all eyes on Rafah" are examples of antisemitic hate speech.

On Thursday a judge ruled that Tufts University student Rümeysa Öztürk shall be transferred to the state of Vermont as the Trump administration fights to deport her. Öztürk's sole offense is having written an op-ed in the university paper mildly denouncing Israel's atrocities in Gaza.

This all comes as a new poll finds that a majority of Americans oppose the Trump administration's new policy of deporting foreigners for expressing wrongthink about Israel. They're taking away the right of US citizens to hear what Israel's critics have to say, and they are doing so directly against the will of the US citizens themselves.

There's a video that Israel apologists are sharing around which they claim shows pro-Palestine activists blocking Jewish students from walking through the campus of Yale University, and it's just so illustrative of the fake "antisemitism" crisis we're being told necessitates the elimination of free speech rights throughout all of western civilization.

If you watch the clip you can see a student wearing a kippah being filmed by someone behind him and demanding to walk directly through what appears to be a relatively small group of activists in the midst of an anti-genocide demonstration. The demonstrators are heard telling him to walk around them, which is what any normal person does when they wish to be on the other side of a physical human body (or indeed any physical object), and you can clearly see people walking around them in the background of the video.

This is like walking up to a cheer squad in the middle of a human pyramid, demanding to walk through them, and then claiming they refused to do so because they hate your religion. It's just so transparently bat shit insane, but it's being shared around in all seriousness by Zionist pundits and politicians as a sign of an antisemitism crisis at a prominent university. This is the kind of evidence that's being cited for the need to stomp out free speech in our society.

I'm going to keep saying it and saying it until the message gets through: Zionism is the single greatest threat to free speech in the western world today. Nothing is eroding people's rights to free expression faster than the support that western governments have for the apartheid state of Israel and the atrocities it is committing.

This isn't just about Gaza now. It's not just about some strangers in the middle east. It's about you. It's about your rights. It's about your right to tell the truth, even if the truth makes your leaders feel uncomfortable.

Even if you are not a sufficiently moral and compassionate person to oppose a genocide on its own merit, at this point you should at least be opposing the erosion of your own personal liberties for your own sake.

•

Nobody Say "Fuck Israel, Free Palestine"

Nobody say "Fuck Israel, Free Palestine." Saying "Fuck Israel, Free Palestine" is very offensive to people who think genocide is good.

When you say "Fuck Israel, Free Palestine," you are hurting the feelings of the people who believe it's fine to bomb every hospital in Gaza. So you must never, ever say "Fuck Israel, Free Palestine."

Who do you think you are, saying "Fuck Israel, Free Palestine"? Don't you know that by saying "Fuck Israel, Free Palestine" you are causing the people who applaud the deliberate starvation of an entire civilian population to become emotionally upset?

Instead of saying "Fuck Israel, Free Palestine," you should try putting yourself in the shoes of the tender-hearted individuals who support the complete ethnic cleansing of the Palestinian people. They're just minding their own business, merrily celebrating the carpet bombing of a giant concentration camp full of children, and then you come along and ruin their day by saying "Fuck Israel, Free Palestine"? What a cruel and hateful thing that would be.

I mean, all they are doing is cheerleading the mutilation, evisceration and incineration of children, and the assassination of journalists and medical workers, and the systematic destruction of civilian infrastructure, and the complete flattening of an entire region whose population they are methodically exterminating via bullets, bombs, starvation and disease. It's not like they're doing anything nasty or disgusting like saying offensive words. Offensive words like "Fuck Israel, Free Palestine."

So don't say "Fuck Israel, Free Palestine." Under no circumstances should anyone ever say "Fuck Israel, Free Palestine." And they must certainly never say "Fuck Israel, Free Palestine" as many times as they possibly can, every single day until Palestine is free, and get everyone else to say it constantly as well.

Again, the phrase you must avoid saying at all cost is Fuck Israel, Free Palestine.

Fuck Israel, Free Palestine.

Fearure image via Adobe Stock.

All The Worst Evils Are Happening Right Out In The Open

Trump is committing genocide for Israel after publicly admitting to being bought and owned by the Adelsons.

All the worst shit happens right out in the open. You don't need to come up with any elaborate conspiracy theories to see it. It's right there, completely unhidden.

It's not hidden, it's just spun. Disguised by the propaganda of the mass media who frame this holocaust as a war of defense in response to a terrorist attack while constantly diverting our attention to other far less significant issues.

It says so much about the power of the imperial propaganda machine that Trump could openly admit to having been fully controlled by Adelson cash on the campaign trail, get elected, and then facilitate a blatant extermination campaign in Gaza while aggressively stomping out free speech that is critical of Israel throughout the United States — and somehow not have this be the main thing that everyone talks about all the time. It is only because our minds are being forcefully manipulated by the powerful at mass scale that this has been the case.

The narrative spin is greatly aided by the fact that Trump isn't doing much different from the previous president here. A public which has been indoctrinated from childhood into seeing everything in Democrat-vs-Republican binaries is conditioned to focus far more on the differences between the two parties than the similarities. But you can learn a whole lot more about real power and what's actually going on in the world by paying less attention to how US presidents differ from each other, and more attention to the ways in which they are the same.

The mass-scale psychological manipulation is so pervasive and ubiquitous that only a small minority are reacting to history's first live-streamed genocide with an appropriate level of horror. If Americans could see what their government is doing in their name with fresh eyes and uncallused

hearts, the nation's capitol would be burnt to the ground within days. But because their vision is clouded by propaganda indoctrination they can't see it, so they overlook what's right in front of them while awaiting a gigantic Epstein bombshell or UFO disclosure or some other Big Reveal that never comes.

Consider the possibility that the Big Reveal has already happened. That it's been right here staring you in the face this entire time, but you haven't noticed its significance because it has been constantly normalized for you throughout your life since you were small. That the truth behind all your most sparkly conspiracy theories could be published online tomorrow, and it still wouldn't tell you as much about what your rulers are doing and how evil they are as what's already happening in plain sight.

This is the dystopia we were warned about. It's not some ominous threat looming on the horizon. It's here. We are being psychologically manipulated at mass scale into consenting to the most nightmarish atrocities imaginable. Children's bodies are being shredded to bits right in front of us. And when you turn on the TV you see famous people laughing and making jokes with fake plastic grins, babbling about vapid nonsense. This is the dystopia. It isn't on its way. It's here.

We don't need a Big Reveal. If the Big Reveal happened next week, the public would be indoctrinated into overlooking and dismissing it by the imperial spin machine by the weekend. We don't need new information, we need people to truly see the information that's already here. To see it with eyes that are free from the cataracts of propaganda conditioning, with hearts that are free from the calluses of desensitization. Waking the public up is less about whistleblowers, FOIA requests and investigative journalism at this point than it is about finding creative and artistic ways to get people noticing

the information that's already public.

And the good news is that we can all help do this. We can all help our fellow members of the public to see what's really happening with fresh eyes. Using our creativity, our humor, our insight and our compassion, we can find new ways every day to open a new pair of eyelids to the truth of our present circumstances.

Our rulers do not have creativity. They do not have humor, insight or compassion. These are not tools that they have in their toolbox, and they have no weapons to counter them. All they have is manipulation, and manipulation only works if you don't know it's happening to you. Our task is to keep finding new and creative ways to help more people see and understand the ways in which they have been manipulated.

Feature image by UNRWA via Wikimedia Commons.

We Are Trapped In A Dystopia That Is Ruled By Lunatics
•Notes From The Edge Of The Narrative Matrix•

We really need a name for the mental illness that comes with obscene amounts of wealth. Elon Musk's bizarre progeny obsession. All the weird shit Michael Jackson did. The stories you hear about rich families making their servants clean their toilets after every use or throw away plates after every meal.

Call it rich-brain or something. That psychological phenomenon where extreme wealth causes people to lose their mental moorings and spin off into deep space because there's no one in their lives telling them "no" or holding them to any standards of normal human behavior. Where their ability to shape their day to day lives however they want with no limitations lets them fly off into uncharted psychological territory where they'll have whole teams of people orchestrating elaborate scenes and projects to accommodate their debilitating neuroses.

We need a good label for this phenomenon because these are the individuals who are shaping our world. Many people suffering from psychological disorders will come up with unhealthy ideas for how society ought to be run, but they don't have the means to turn their vision into a reality. The people who are made insane by obscene amounts of wealth are not restricted in this way. Their mental illnesses can actually directly influence how human civilization plays out on this planet.

As billionaires take more and more control over our world, we are finding ourselves increasingly led by those least qualified to lead us. We are trapped in a dystopia that is ruled by lunatics. We should probably do something about that.

•

They're ripping kids in half right in front of us and telling us we need to be mad at Kneecap and Ms Rachel.

•

A Palestine supporter witnesses new footage every day of children being mutilated, shredded and burned to death by Israel. An Israel supporter spends every day avoiding looking at that same footage. This one fact tells you very clearly who is on the wrong side of history here.

•

When you witness an injustice you can either oppose it, look away, or make up some reason why the injustice is okay. Only the first option can lead to the cessation of the injustice. Ignoring the Gaza holocaust looks different from justifying it, but both yield the same result.

There are people opposing the genocide and there are people justifying it, but the largest group by far are those standing in the middle and shrugging. These people may tell themselves that they are morally superior to the ones actively cheerleading a mass atrocity, and at first glance this may appear to be the case, but in practice both are choosing an option that allows the mass atrocity to continue. One is just more photogenic than the other. It allows a certain type of person to feel nice about themselves while still facilitating an active genocide.

This is almost everyone with the loudest and most influential voices in our society today, by the way. The celebrities. The people with the largest platforms. Most of them are not actively supporting the Gaza holocaust, they're just sitting there watching it happen, like a psychopath sitting back watching a toddler drown to death in a swimming pool. They know something terrible is happening, but they know they'll pay a professional price if they oppose it, so they avail themselves of the many distractions afforded to the wealthy and keep their attention fixed on the insignificant.

And the end result is that this nightmare continues. Day after day. Month after month. Year after year. Because too many people, when faced with history's first live-streamed genocide, have chosen to do nothing.

•

It would be a mistake to view the Chinese people's skyrocketing quality of life as miraculous or extraordinary. Beijing made some very clever decisions over the years, but ultimately it's just doing the normal thing: spending the nation's wealth on the public instead of on war.

•

When capitalism simps want to shit on China they call it communist. When they want to dismiss its accomplishments they say it only happened because China became capitalist. When you ask why your country can't do what China is doing in order to share those same accomplishments they circle back around to "No, that's communism!" again.

•

And meanwhile the war in Ukraine rages on, for no reason other than the fact that under our psychotic status quo it is much easier to start a war than to end one.

The risk of nuclear war is far lower than it was in the early months of the conflict, but Ukrainian lives are still being thrown into a proxy war to no one's benefit but the war profiteers. NATO's never going to directly enter the war, and without a massive escalation on that level it's inevitable that this thing ends with a peace deal where Ukraine has to give up a fair amount of land. At this point it's just a bunch of men killing each other and blowing each other's limbs off for no good reason while they wait for that conclusion to arrive, because a bunch of corrupt bureaucrats far away from the fighting keep postponing it.

It's so, so ugly and so, so stupid. Such a pointless, idiotic thing for all this suffering and dying to be happening for. This whole nightmare could have been avoided with a little diplomacy and a few low-cost concessions from the US empire, but they decided to provoke a war to move a few pieces around on the grand chessboard for the advancement of their goal of planetary domination instead.

The world is ruled by sociopaths.

•

I keep meaning to mention that watching or listening to Dave DeCamp's half-hour show for Antiwar News every day is the easiest way to cultivate a lucid understanding of what's going on in the world. Just put it on over breakfast or on your way to work or whatever and you'll always understand what the empire is up to from day to day.

Other good resources include:

Antiwar.com

Breakthrough News

Consortium News

Drop Site News and its quality Twitter account

World Socialist Website

Electronic Intifada

Mintpress News

The Grayzone

The Cradle

Moon of Alabama

Responsible Statecraft

•

It's Always About The System
•Notes From The Edge Of The Narrative Matrix•

The main reason more people don't just go all in with opposing the US empire and rejecting all its propaganda about enemy states is because they can't handle working through the heavy cognitive dissonance which comes with recognizing that everything you've been taught is a lie.

Most people recognize to some extent that the US and its allies do bad things, but those who take it all the way into a clear understanding that this power structure is responsible for most of our world's ills are a small minority in the west. Even the relatively awake ones will try to cling on to this or that imperial propaganda narrative about nations like China, North Korea, Iran and/or Russia. Most try to at least keep a foot in the door of their imperial indoctrination, so they don't have to experience the psychological discomfort of letting it close completely.

But that's where the truth is. Coming to a lucid understanding of the world necessarily means abandoning all untruths for truth on every level. If you can work up the courage to really do this, the entire mainstream western worldview gets flushed right down the toilet.

•

Israel is a bad country full of bad people. They are not bad because of their religion, they are bad because they live in a genocidal apartheid state whose existence depends on indoctrinating its people into seeing genocide and apartheid as good. It's the system.

It's always the system. Western countries are full of shitty people with shitty beliefs who do shitty things to each other all the time. This isn't because westerners are inherently shitty, nor because humans are inherently shitty. It's because here in the western empire we live under capitalism, which encourages selfish behavior and cutthroat competition against each other, and because we are indoctrinated into accepting the tyrannical white supremacist propaganda of western imperialism.

Nobody is inherently bad. We are all the products of our conditioning, and the systems under which we live play a large role in shaping our conditioning. That's what mass media propaganda and the indoctrination of western schooling are: streamlined systems for determining what our conditioning will be. These systems can have as much of an effect on our view of the world as other forms of conditioning like trauma.

The powerful understand that humans are an easily conditioned animal, and so vast resources are poured into determining what our conditioning shall be. As soon as we are old enough to start learning about the world our minds are trained to shape us into good cogs in the imperial machine. Good employees and gear-turners for capitalism. Good soldiers and police officers. Good citizens who would never do anything to inconvenience our rulers.

We are funneled through carefully crafted factories of conditioning by the malignant systems under which we live. As long as those malignant systems exist they will keep churning out malignant people, and goodness will struggle to find any purchase. This is true whether you are talking about capitalism, imperialism, or Zionism.

•

I'm the least religious person I know but some westerners are getting so obnoxious about Islam and Muslims that I sometimes think about converting, just to piss them off.

•

Had a medical incident in my family the other day. It's funny what a reminder of human mortality can do to dispel all the little resentments and dramas that can build up between loved ones over the years and cause all the old grievances to be seen for the insignificant mind fluff that they are.

And right now I feel sorrowful that it so often takes a major health scare or accident to remind us of this. We all know we're all going to die, but we let the small stuff come between us anyway. We let the little quibbles in our heads stop us from touching hands and experiencing intimacy with each other during our fleeting time on this beautiful planet.

In the play Waiting for Godot, Beckett writes that our mothers "give birth astride of a grave," and it's just so true.

"They give birth astride of a grave, the light gleams an instant, then it's night once more," the character Pozzo laments.

The line resonates because that really is what the human experience feels like. We get a short time here, and then we're gone.

How bizarre is it, then, that we still find time to hate each other? That we still have time for grudges and resentment? That our mothers give birth astride of a grave, and we punch and kick each other on the way down?

Bukowski said, "We're all going to die, all of us, what a circus! That alone should make us love each other but it doesn't. We are terrorized and flattened by trivialities, we are eaten up by nothing."

It's about the weirdest thing you could possibly imagine.

Feature image via Adobe Stock.

Biden Never Pushed For A Ceasefire In Gaza
•Notes From The Edge Of The Narrative Matrix•

Former Israeli ambassador to the United States Mike Herzog acknowledged on Israeli media on Sunday that the Biden administration never at any time pressured Israel for a ceasefire in Gaza.

"God did the State of Israel a favor that Biden was the president during this period, because it could have been much worse," Herzog said. "We fought [in Gaza] for over a year and the administration never came to us and said, 'ceasefire now.' It never did."

So everyone who said the Biden administration was working for a ceasefire lied. They lied that whole entire time. They committed genocide and lied about it, and then they said you were crazy and irresponsible if you didn't support them.

People's rage should shake heaven and earth.

•

The US has committed another huge massacre of civilians in Yemen, this time bombing a detention center full of African migrants in Saada. Some 68 people have reportedly been killed, making this Trump's worst massacre in Yemen since his terrorist attack on a Hodeida fuel port killed 80 people earlier this month.

Trump's massacres of civilians in Saada and Hodeida are much more evil than anything he has done in the United States domestically, but they've received almost no attention from the media or from Democrats because in the eyes of the empire Yemenis don't count as human beings and killing them is normal.

•

The word "antisemite" has become so meaningless that whenever someone uses it you have to ask them "What kind? The Hitler-was-right kind or the stop-bombing-hospitals kind?"

•

It's absolutely bat shit insane that it's increasingly illegal to voice any praise for groups like Hamas and Hezbollah in the UK and Australia just because the government deems them "terrorists". What happens when the government is wrong and one of those groups is right?

•

They're seriously going to ethnically cleanse Gaza after a monstrous extermination campaign and then look us all dead in the eyes and tell us we need to hate China.

•

It's wild how the US and Israel just came right out and said "Yeah we're working on permanently ethnically cleansing all Palestinians from the Gaza Strip," and then the entire western political/media class went right back to pretending to believe this is about fighting Hamas.

•

Calling the Gaza genocide a "war" is like seeing a man beating a toddler to death and calling it a "fight".

So much evil hides behind calling this thing a war. If you accept that it's a war then you have to take seriously arguments like "It's a war, civilians die in war," or "Hamas shouldn't have started a war they can't win." If it's a war then it has two sides who share comparable levels of responsibility for any bad things that happen during that time. If it's a war then it's taken as a given that Israel's primary target is Hamas, and not the civilian population of Gaza in its entirety.

But it's not a war, it's a naked ethnic cleansing operation being carried out by a highly sophisticated military with the backing of the most powerful empire that has ever existed. It's a globe-spanning power structure openly purging a Palestinian territory of Palestinian life using a full siege and the systematic destruction of all healthcare and civilian infrastructure, being resisted by a few thousand guys with homemade rockets and dwindling supplies. That's not a "war". It's not even a "conflict". It's a slaughter. It's a holocaust.

If the Gaza holocaust is a "war", then shooting fish in a barrel is "hunting". Beating up a quadriplegic is a "street brawl". A SWAT team shooting an unarmed civilian is a "gun fight". No conflicts are perfectly equal, but past a certain level of one-sidedness the language of conflict becomes absurd. The daily massacres we are seeing in Gaza are far beyond that point.

They are raining military explosives on top of a giant concentration camp packed full of children while deliberately starving the entire civilian population to death. They have complete control over the enclave, and they are using that control to eradicate the presence of Palestinians in Gaza. That is not war. That is genocide.

Feature image by The White House via Wikimedia Commons.

Israel's Backers Keep Whining That They're Losing Control Of The Narrative

Amnesty International is now calling Israel's mass atrocity in Gaza "a live-streamed genocide" due to the way this nightmare is unfolding right in front of us on the screens of our devices around the world, and public support for Israel is plummeting in the United States.

Zionists are losing control of the narrative, and they know it. And they are not taking it well.

During a speech at a summit hosted by the Jewish News Syndicate earlier this week, former US senator Norm Coleman said that Jews are "the masters of the universe" and should use their power in Silicon Valley to control online information in order to win a "digital war".

Coleman, who is Jewish, made the following remarks on Monday:

> "A majority of Gen Z have an unfavorable impression of Israel. And, my friends, I think the reason for that is that we're losing the digital war. They're getting their information from TikTok... and we're losing that war.

> "And when you think about it, the masters of the universe are Jews! We've got Altman at OpenAI, we've got [Facebook founder Mark] Zuckerberg, we've got [Google founder] Sergey Brin, we've got a group across the board. Jan Koum, y'know, founded WhatsApp. It's us.

> "And we have to figure out a way to win the digital battle. We've got to get our digital sneakers on, so that the truth can prevail over the lies. And when we do that, the future of Israel will be stronger because a majority of all Americans will support Israel. We'll make that happen, we have to make it happen."

If any anti-Zionist with a public profile had said Jews control Silicon Valley and use it to influence public opinion for the benefit of Israel, they'd be forcefully denounced by the entire western political-media class as a rabid antisemite. But a Jewish politician saying Jews must use their control over Silicon Valley to influence public opinion about Israel receives no attention from that same political-media class.

Interestingly, at that same event, Meta's "Jewish Diaspora" chief Jordana Cutler noted that Meta platforms like Facebook and Instagram "banned content claiming Zionists run the world or control the media." Under Cutler's own guidelines, the prior comments from her fellow attendee would have been banned if he had said them on Facebook instead of at the Jewish News Syndicate International Policy Summit.

Israel's backers have been whining about losing control of the narrative for months.

In February, US Senator Lindsey Graham told the press at an event in Tel Aviv that in the Arab world "Israel has won the war on the ground, but they've lost it on television," lamenting that "all they see is morning, noon and night attacks on the Palestinian people."

The Arab world is seeing attacks on the Palestinian people morning noon and night because that is what's happening. That is what the entire world is seeing.

In a talk at the McCain Institute last year, then-Senator Mitt Romney told then-Secretary of State Antony Blinken that Congress supports banning TikTok because it shares information that turns people's opinions against Israel, saying such information has a "very, very challenging effect on the narrative."

After bemoaning Israel's lack of success at "PR" regarding its Gaza assault, Romney just came right out and said that this was "why there was such overwhelming support for us to shut down potentially TikTok or other entities of that nature" — with "us" meaning himself and his fellow lawmakers on Capitol Hill.

"How this narrative has evolved, yeah, it's a great question," Blinken responded, saying that at the beginning of his career in Washington everyone was getting their information from television and physical newspapers like The New York Times, The Wall Street Journal and The Washington Post.

"Now, of course, we are on an intravenous feed of information with new impulses, inputs every millisecond," Blinken continued. "And of course, the way this has played out on social media has dominated the narrative. And you have a social media ecosystem environment in which context, history, facts get lost, and the emotion, the impact of images dominates. And we can't — we can't discount that, but I think it also has a very, very, very challenging effect on the narrative."

Notice how he said the word "narrative" three times? That's how empire managers talk to each other, because that's how they think about everything. Everything is about narrative control. It doesn't matter what happens as long as you can control how people think about what happens.

During the university protests last year, Palantir CEO Alex Karp came right out and said that if those on the side of the protesters win the debate on this issue, the west will lose the ability to wage wars.

"We kind of just think these things that are happening, across college campuses especially, are like a sideshow — no, they are the show," Karp said during his rant. "Because if we lose the intellectual debate, you will not be able to deploy any army in the west, ever."

In an audio recording published by the Tehran Times in 2023, Anti-Defamation League CEO Jonathan Greenblatt is heard saying "We really have a TikTok problem" and calling for more aggressive online narrative operations to control public opinion about Israel among young people.

In the audio recording, whose authenticity was confirmed by the ADL, Greenblatt says the following:

"I also wanna point out that we have a major major major generational problem. All the polling that I've seen, ADL's polling, ICC's polling, independent polling suggests this is not a left or right gap, folks. The issue in United States' support for Israel is not left and right: it is young and old. And the numbers of young people who think that Hamas's you know massacre was justified is shockingly and terrifyingly high. And so we really have a Tik-Tok problem, a Gen-Z problem, that our community needs to put the same brains that gave us Taglit, the same brains that gave us all these other amazing innovations, need to put our energy toward this like, fast. Cause again like we've been chasing this left-right divide. It's the wrong game. The real game is the next generation, and the Hamas and their accomplices, the useful idiots in the West, are falling in line in ways that are terrifying."

Israel's backers are losing control of the narrative because there's only so much that PR spin can do to convince people they're not seeing what's right in front of their eyes. If you're strangling someone right in front of me there are no words you can say to me to convince me I'm not seeing someone being strangled, no matter how skillful you are at manipulation.

Actions speak louder than words. Talk is cheap. A picture is worth a thousand words. These aphorisms exist for a reason. Past a certain point there is only so much that mountains of verbiage can accomplish when people are seeing history's first live-streamed genocide playing out right before their eyes.

Whoever controls the narrative controls the world. The average human life is dominated by mental stories, so if you can control the stories they are telling about what's going on, you can control the humans.

Losing narrative control is losing real power. That's why Israel's supporters are growing increasingly anxious.

Feature image via Gage Skidmore (CC BY-SA 2.0)

https://www.caitlinjohnst.one

www.ingramcontent.com/pod-product-compliance
Lightning Source LLC
Chambersburg PA
CBHW050241290326
41930CB00043B/3272